English Yellow-Glazed Earthenware

English Yellow-Glazed Earthenware

J. JEFFERSON MILLER II

BARRIE & JENKINS LONDON

in association with Smithsonian Institution Press, Washington, DC, USA

© Barrie & Jenkins, London 1974

First published 1974 by Barrie & Jenkins Ltd.
24 Highbury Crescent, London N15 1RX
in association with Smithsonian Institution
Press, Washington, DC, USA

ISBN 0 214 20008 6

Printed in Great Britain at Chapel River Press, Andover, Hants

For Anne Miller, my personal curator

CONTENTS

Acknowledgements

In the preparation of this book the part played by Mr and Mrs Jack L. Leon was paramount. First, the Leons assembled the collection. During a decade of intense collecting activity they developed contacts among collectors, dealers, curators, and ceramic historians. These associations, in turn, led to information which has been incorporated in this book. The Leons were never collectors in a limited sense; frequently they conducted their own investigations, the fruits of which were unselfishly provided to me.

Among the many individuals whose advice and suggestions helped this study to become a book, a few merit special mention. They are John Austin, Curator of Ceramics, Colonial Williamsburg; Robert Charleston, Keeper of Ceramics, Victoria & Albert Museum; W. J. Grant-Davidson, Honorary Curator of Ceramics, Royal Institution of South Wales; Vivian Scheidemantel Hawes, former Associate Curator of Decorative Arts, the Art Institute of Chicago; Dwight P. Lanmon, Assistant Curator, Henry Francis du Pont Winterthur Museum; Emily Manheim, D. M. & P. Manheim Antiques Corporation; Arnold Mountford, Director, City Museum and Art Gallery, Stoke-on-Trent; Alan Smith, former Keeper of Ceramics and Applied Art, City of Liverpool Museums; Ross E. Taggart, Senior Curator, William Rockhill Nelson Gallery of Art, and Donald Towner, Honorary Secretary of the English Ceramic Circle.

Within the National Museum of History and Technology of the Smithsonian Institution, Washington, DC, I received special encouragement from Robert G. Tillotson, Assistant Director, and John H. White, Jr, Chairman of the Department of Industries. Robert P. Multhauf, Senior Scientific Scholar, Department of Science and Technology, provided guidance in the history of eighteenth- and nineteenth-century chemistry. Renee Altman typed the manuscript, assisted in research and made order out of chaos. Jennifer Oka supervised the photography and maintained a complicated photographic file. The photography was done in the Photography Laboratory of the National Museum of History and Technology. To all of these people, I express deep appreciation.

Foreword

There have been yellow wares since time immemorial. The Chinese made them and yellow-ground porcelain was made by the Meissen factory and at Worcester, Chelsea, Derby and elsewhere in England. One can even find saltglaze wares with a yellow ground. Lovely lead-glazed wares in the Astbury manner were made in a soft ochreous yellow in the middle of the eighteenth century. Wedgwood invented a yellow glaze for his pineapple and melon wares, but none of these constitutes the class of ware collected by Mr and Mrs Jack Leon and here described so admirably by Mr J. Jefferson Miller II.

The wares which form the subject of this book were produced by a number of English potteries during the late eighteenth and early nineteenth centuries. This was a period when great changes of outlook were taking place. Technical abilities had never been so high and in pottery there were a great many innovations. Decoration underwent a radical change. The free decorative enamelling of the eighteenth century gave way to cheaper and more mechanical processes mostly involving the use of slips and glazes. Among all these innovations we find one in which a creamware or pearlware was coated with an overall yellow glaze sometimes with the addition of enamelling, transfer-printing, lustre or other embellishments and this is the special corner of English ceramics which will be explored in this book—a subject never tackled before except in the most cursory manner.

Yellow as a colour in ceramics has always been sought after by collectors. Yellow-ground porcelain is among the most costly on the market today and many of the yellow earthenwares discussed in this book, though by no means competing in this respect, are nevertheless significant in their own right. My own preference is for the plain yellow wares without the addition of any further ornament, with the possible exception of just a touch of enamelling, such as in the few pieces known to have been produced by the Leeds Pottery. The two melon tureens in plate **XXXVIII** are examples of this, and also a superb coffee pot in the Yorkshire Museum. Some examples seem to me to have been spoilt by the introduction of too many different types of decoration on the same piece— very ingenious, no doubt, but to my mind showing a lack of good taste, though one must remember the class of society for which they were made. The great majority of these yellow-glazed wares were undoubtedly made for use and decoration in cottages and smaller dwellings where a spot of clear yellow would brighten a dingy mantelpiece or dresser.

I would like to commend this book as being an important addition to the general repertoire of ceramic studies, for not only does it discuss the yellow wares, their history and origins, but it also forms a miniature history of English pottery of the period, written with considerable insight and knowledge.

Donald C. Towner, London 1973

Hon. Secretary, English Ceramic Circle

Introduction

MAKING A COLLECTION by Jack & Eleanor Leon

In 1962, in London, we acquired a mug decorated with hand-painted flowers and leaves. The background was a lovely bright yellow. This was the beginning of a collection of yellow-glazed English earthenware that presently numbers over six hundred pieces.

There is merit in forming a collection over a very long period of time. Common mistakes can usually be avoided if knowledge of the subject is acquired before collecting has gone too far. Yet our collection of yellow-glazed English earthenware was acquired in a comparatively short period. We had found the incentive to collect but felt the urgency of time and wished we had been twenty years younger. Although we still search for rare and unusual pieces, the basis of the collection was formed in less than ten years.

Again and again we are asked the question: 'How did you become interested in this particular type of pottery?' The questioner would probably like to hear of a fascinating experience which led us into this field, but the truth is that it was all very routine.

Until the time we bought our first few pieces, we were not aware that English potters had at times used an overall yellow glaze. The colour appealed to us and the first forms we saw had a simplicity of decoration that we considered special. We had no idea then that we were on our way to becoming serious collectors of this earthenware or that we had singled out a relatively scarce type of ceramic. In our initial enthusiasm we searched in London and other areas of England for additional pieces, only to realize that they were difficult to find. It became a challenge when we found that our trips through the English countryside led us to lovely villages and scenery, but little yellow-glazed earthenware. After several treks into various parts of England we decided our approach had to be changed.

When dealers were asked about the yellow glaze, they invariably said: 'Oh, you mean canary yellow', or some would call it 'canary lustre', adding 'Sorry, we just don't see much of it.'

Subsequently we found the designation 'yellow glaze' in one of the old Leeds Pottery pattern books, and the same descriptive term for recipes using this colour in early nineteenth-century records of the Herculaneum Pottery, Liverpool. It became apparent that 'canary' was a misnomer, or at least misleading, since there is a wide variation in the yellow background colour. Sometimes it is true canary, but there are many pieces that are sulphur yellow, some almost a mustard colour, and others almost as pale as ivory. We have made an effort to have the description 'yellow-glazed earthenware' adopted generally; the word 'lustre' correctly applies only to those yellow-glazed pieces actually decorated with lustre.

After these first explorations we decided to form a small collection, though we had very little idea of how to go about it. Returning home from England we visited dealers in the United States, but again with meagre results. It took us a year to learn that only certain dealers handled this ware, here and in England. If we were to acquire a collection our best approach was to make contact with these dealers and rely on them to advise us what pieces were available. Since this field is a highly specialized one, the method of acquisition differs from that for acquiring many other kinds of English ceramics.

In the hope of increasing our knowledge, we hunted in bookshops dealing in volumes on ceramics, we visited many of the museums in England and the United States which have outstanding English ceramic collections, and we made extensive enquiries about private collections of yellow-glazed ware.

Results were disappointing. Books on English ceramics contain little or no information on yellow-glazed pottery, museums have a minimal number of pieces and we soon found that in all of England apparently only a few small collections existed. Many of the museum curators and authors of books on ceramics whom we consulted were unfamiliar with the subject. We decided we would have to do our own research, using whatever help we might get from the very co-operative people we had met during our brief involvement with collecting. Our interest was heightened by this challenge. In considering the formation of a comprehensive collection, it occurred to us that it could conceivably be the first of its kind, and the possibility of combining collecting with original research then became our objective.

Eventually we contacted two owners of yellow-glazed earthenware collections in England and happily found both to be extremely co-operative. One collection was in Newcastle-upon-Tyne, the other far removed, in Sennen, Cornwall, a few miles from Land's End.

Mr James McHarg in Newcastle-upon-Tyne had a superb collection of pottery and English porcelain, including a small group of yellow-glazed pieces. All of these were lustred and one of the finest was a beautiful two-handled loving cup, now in our collection. We also obtained several other pieces from the McHarg collection which was later sold at Sotheby's. Mr and Mrs McHarg were charming hosts; they told us all they knew about our speciality and served us the most delicious high tea in all of England. We had the pleasure of revisiting them the following year.

Mr McHarg, at our first meeting, suggested we join the English Ceramic Circle and subsequently proposed us for membership. We are extremely grateful to him for this suggestion as we have gained much information from the meetings and the published Transactions of this group. Over the years we have enjoyed a close association with a number of English Ceramic Circle members who have materially added to our knowledge and understanding in the field of English ceramics.

Mr and Mrs T. G. William Fowler of Sennen, Cornwall, invited us to visit them. Their home was full of antiques—ceramics, glass, fascinating objects carved from Cornish stone, and many other things. Mr Fowler was a compulsive collector and quite literally we had to walk through the rooms sideways, crab-fashion, because of cases and tables laden with the results of more than sixty years of collecting. Now, at the age of eighty, Mr Fowler could still recall where he had purchased each piece.

His collection of yellow-glazed pottery consisted of about twenty-five pieces, all in mint condition. Despite the fact that he loved every piece he owned and was always reluctant to part with anything, he became interested in our project and agreed to let us have a few pieces. More than that, he promised he would not dispose of any of his yellow pieces without giving us first refusal. He was as good as his word, and by the time of his death in 1967 we had purchased the lot.

In a field such as English ceramics, which has been widely explored, it is satisfying to make a contribution, no matter how small. Although most English earthenware of the late eighteenth and early nineteenth centuries is unmarked, we did obtain several pieces of yellow-glazed earthenware bearing potters' marks. This was heady stuff and we searched diligently for more. Eventually we found a few pieces bearing the impressed mark WEDGWOOD. By now we were somewhat more knowledgeable about our collection but did not fully realize the true import of this. Shortly thereafter we discovered that, although Wedgwood has a great following, few scholars and collectors, if any (including the Wedgwood factory and museum), had any idea that Wedgwood had used an overall yellow glaze. There are now eleven marked pieces of yellow-glazed Wedgwood in our collection and this we consider to be an important contribution to English ceramic history.

One of the most pleasurable and satisfying experiences we have had is in sharing what we learned with other interested people. We have enjoyed working together on the papers read to various ceramic organizations. Included in these are the China Students' Club of Boston, the Wedgwood Society of New York and of Boston, the Wedgwood International Seminar, and the English Ceramic Study Group of Philadelphia. Our most important opportunity was an invitation to read a paper before the English Ceramic Circle at the Victoria and Albert Museum in 1970, and subsequently having it published in their Transactions for that year. This was the first paper, we believe, that an American had presented to the Circle.

Of the museums we visited in England the great Victoria and Albert, we found to our disappointment, had only one piece of yellow-glazed English earthenware. A few pieces are on display at the Brighton Museum, as part of the Willett Collection, and there is a small group of lustred pieces at the City Museum and Art Gallery, Stoke-on-Trent. We found several pieces at the Yorkshire Museum in York, and at the Laing Museum, Newcastle-upon-Tyne. Although the output of yellow glaze by the Sunderland Potteries was considerable, the museum at Sunderland, which displays only ceramics of the area, did not own a piece. We recently sent them a transfer-printed yellow-glazed jug probably made by the Garrison Pottery of Sunderland. The Liverpool City Museum has a magnificent $16\frac{1}{2}$ inch yellow-glazed jug, decorated with a dozen transfer-printed scenes and hand-coloured over the transfers. In Wales there are several pieces at the Glynn Vivian Museum, Swansea, and a few at the National Museum of Wales in Cardiff. One or two pieces are on display at the Fitzwilliam Museum in Cambridge.

In the United States, several museums have small collections of yellow-glazed English earthenware. The largest of these is in the William Rockhill Nelson Gallery of Art, Kansas City, which has about fifty pieces, all part of the Burnap Collection. The Lucy Maude Buckingham Collection at the Art Institute of Chicago contains some fine yellow-glazed English earthenware, and at Brandeis University, Waltham, Mass., the Rose Museum has a small exhibit of exceptionally fine forms of both English and French earthenware with a yellow glaze.

The major part of our collection is now in the National Museum of History and Technology of the Smithsonian Institution. It is our sincere hope that by making a comprehensive collection readily available to students of ceramics, we will in some small way further the knowledge and interest already existing in this field. Further, we hope others who are not students or collectors will derive pleasure from viewing this collection.

We cannot conclude without expressing our appreciation to all those whose encouragement has been of paramount importance. We are especially indebted to Miss Millie Manheim who made the contact for us with the Smithsonian Institution. Her enthusiasm for the collection and her generous sharing of valuable time and invaluable knowledge constantly spurred us on in our field.

We must surely include more than a mere mention of the Smithsonian Institution itself. A beautiful and unusual exhibit area has been prepared by the National Museum of History and Technology to house our collection. Robert Widder, Senior Designer, Design Division, created the unique architectural design. Our association with him during the planning stage and the construction has ripened into a warm friendship. We are most gratified that this great institution and its curators of ceramics, J. Jefferson Miller II and Paul V. Gardner, have been enthusiastic from the first moment they saw our collection.

The author of this book, Jeff Miller, has had to make his own time—on planes, on short vacations, and at home—to get the text in shape for publication. Additional research had to be done in his very few spare moments. All this was accomplished, much to our amazement, in a minimum of time. It has been our privilege to be associated with him on this project.

In the home of our good friends Helen and Robert Adler in Highland Park, Illinois, we first saw pieces of yellow-glazed earthenware. Indirectly they influenced our interest in this pottery.

One of the pleasures of collecting and doing research is getting to know the people with whom one becomes involved. In discussions with curators, authors writing about ceramics, and ceramic historians, one invariably gains knowledge. We received considerable help, not only about our specialized field, but about English ceramics in general.

We are particularly grateful to Donald C. Towner, author and leading authority on the Leeds Pottery and early cream-coloured earthenware; to Alan Smith, former Keeper of Ceramics and Applied Art at the Liverpool City Museum; to W. J. Grant-Davidson, Hon. Curator of Ceramics, Royal Institution of South Wales; Robert J. Charleston, Keeper of Ceramics, Victoria and Albert Museum, and Arnold R. Mountford, Director, City Museum and Art Gallery, Stoke-on-Trent.

Also, we received close co-operation from George P. Willmot, Keeper of Ceramics, Yorkshire Museum, York; S. Collingwood Stevens, Director, Laing Art Museum, Newcastle-upon-Tyne; Robert Rowe, Director, Temple Newsam Museum, Leeds; David S. Thornton, Art Librarian, Leeds City Library and Art Gallery; James H. Wilson, Chief Assistant Curator, Sunderland Museum and Art Gallery, and Terence A. Lockett, author and specialist on the Bramelds and Rockingham Pottery of Swinton, Yorkshire.

CHAPTER ONE

The yellow glaze

English yellow-glazed earthenware may be defined as a type of creamware or pearlware distinguished by an overall yellow glaze. Most of it was made during the final years of the eighteenth century and the first quarter of the nineteenth century. The origins of English yellow-glazed earthenware are obscure. No contemporary document touching upon the beginnings of this distinctive type of earthenware is known to the author. Further, there appears to be no clear-cut prototype for the yellow-glazed wares.

On occasion the evolution of a new ceramic style can be traced in detail. Documentary sources as well as surviving pieces may permit the construction of a valid background of origins and influences. But sometimes the ceramic historian is left without any substantial information in the form of written records or objects, and this is especially true when he attempts to deal with the humbler wares. With a few notable exceptions, potters were far from eloquent and were seldom given to literary exertions. In most cases pottery records, account books, correspondence, and technical data have not been preserved. These general comments are applicable to eighteenth- and early nineteenth-century England. Though many books have been written about English ceramics of the period, factual information concerning stylistic origins is relatively meagre. The historian is left with a jigsaw puzzle. The puzzle can, to some degree, be put together on the basis of comparisons with other aspects of the period's material culture. For example, Georgian silver shapes are found in Chelsea and Bow porcelain, earlier Meissen figures were clearly copied by several English factories, and Japanese designs are discernible in some of the productions of Worcester, Chelsea, Bow, and Longton Hall. When searching for the origins of English yellow-glazed earthenware it is necessary to consider a broad spectrum of seventeenth- and eighteenth-century ceramics. The following thoughts on antecedents, however, can only be offered as possible explanations.

The coarse lead-glazed earthenwares of medieval England were sometimes covered with a yellow glaze. Though dark brown and green glazes were more common, yellow lead glazes were still used during the Tudor period. By the seventeenth century, slip decorating was well established and was to become an increasingly important part of the country's ceramic tradition. Some contemporary observations on the use of the 'yellow' slip were made by Dr Robert Plot in his *Natural History of Staffordshire,* first published in 1686.[1] The Staffordshire slipwares of the late seventeenth- and early eighteenth-centuries included ordinary table and hearthside utilitarian pieces as well as elaborate dishes or chargers made, most probably, for decorative purposes alone. The light-coloured slip grounds varied from cream to yellow. A number of the outstanding large dishes from this period, produced by such famous potters as the Tofts, had yellow slip grounds. A distinctive type, also frequently using yellow slip as a ground colour, was the earthenware from North Devon. The seventeenth- and eighteenth-century North Devon pottery consisted of a gravel-tempered redware, covered with a bright yellow slip. Decoration was achieved by cutting a design (usually stylized foliate or geometric patterns) through the yellow slip to the contrasting red clay body. The effectiveness of the sgraffito decoration on these North Devon wares was enhanced by the dramatic contrast between the design in red and the strong yellow ground.

During the eighteenth century utilitarian slipwares made in Staffordshire and other parts of England were exported in large amounts to the colonies. A number of advertisements in colonial newspapers offered English 'yellow' wares for sale. It is probable that the type of ceramics being advertised was English slipware; until the 1760s the term was also applied to cream-coloured earthenware. For example, in 1757 a New York merchant offered for sale '. . . Crates Common yellow Wares both cups and Dishes . . .'.[2] Another New York vendor, in 1768, advertised 'yellow Dishes by the Crates . . .'.[3] The ubiquity of these yellow slipwares is attested by the many surviving examples as well as the results of archaeological investigations in England and North America.

In addition to the slipwares, one other category of English earthenware should be considered. These are the part yellow-glazed earthenwares moulded in imitation of fruits and vegetables which were probably first produced by Josiah Wedgwood at the time of, or shortly after, the conclusion of his brief partnership (1754-9) with Thomas Whieldon. During the final years of this association, Wedgwood carefully experimented in an attempt to achieve a

1. Robert Plot, *The Natural History of Staffordshire* (Oxford 1686), p.122.
2. Advertisement of Edward Nicoll in *The New York Gazette or the Weekly Post-Boy,* 14 February 1757. Reprinted in Rita S. Gottesman, compiler, *The Arts and Crafts in New York, 1726-1776* (New York Historical Society, New York 1938), pp.90-1.
3. Advertisement of Groves and Stonehouse in the *New York Journal or the General Advertizer,* 24 March 1768. Reprinted in Gottesman, p.89. This second advertisement (of 1768) could have been for creamwares which also seem to have been termed 'yellow wares' at times. See also Ivor Noël Hume, 'Creamware to Pearlware: A Williamsburg Perspective', *Ceramics in America* (Univ. Press of Va., 1973), p.230.

finer green lead glaze for use over cream-coloured earthenware. At the same period, he applied himself to the development of a bright yellow glaze. His success with green and yellow glazes can be measured today by the surviving pieces made in imitation of cauliflowers, melons, cabbages, and pineapples. The bright yellow of the melon and pineapple imitations certainly represented a departure from the more subdued colours of the typical lead-glazed wares manufactured in Staffordshire at that time. Of course, Wedgwood probably was not the only Staffordshire potter seeking better green and yellow glazes. Perhaps the true significance of the new green and yellow wares does not lie in any conjecture as to their place in the chain of influence leading to the development of the overall yellow-glazed wares. Rather, the question of Josiah Wedgwood's hard-headed business motivations may be a more relevant factor. Writing of Wedgwood's experiments, Wolf Mankowitz has stated, 'Wedgwood's challenge to the declining Staffordshire market at this time was the novelty, green and yellow glazed wares'.[4] It seems reasonable to posit that, in a like manner, the inception and continued production of English overall yellow-glazed earthenwares is explicable in terms of an attempt to produce an appealing, colourful product which would sell well at home and abroad.

In considering antecedents, a number of other ceramics that might have had some bearing on the subject should be taken into account. Chinese porcelains with yellow grounds were made as early as the Sung dynasty. During the later Ming dynasty, especially fine porcelains with yellow grounds and contrasting blue decoration were produced during the reign of Hsüan-te (1426-35). The colour continued to be employed during the K'ang Hsi period, and indeed throughout the eighteenth and nineteenth centuries. Some Chinese porcelains with yellow grounds were exported to the West, but logic dictates that the *famille jaune* influenced the fine porcelain factories of Europe rather than the far more prosaic makers of English earthenwares. One most interesting similarity between *famille jaune* porcelains and the English yellow-glazed wares should be noted. Frequently the *famille jaune* wares were given an *overall* yellow enamel ground (inside as well as outside). Such was not the case with many of the other yellow ceramics discussed in the following paragraphs, and the distinction between a glaze and a ground colour should always be kept in mind.

Faience from the eighteenth-century potteries of continental Europe was usually glazed in varying shades of white. At times, ground colours—especially blue and yellow—were used. In Germany, Abstbessingen, Fulda, and Braunschweig potteries, among others, produced faience with yellow grounds, overpainted in other colours. French faience manufacturers, including Moustiers and Samadet, occasionally employed yellow grounds with striking effects.

The eighteenth century was the golden age of porcelain-making in Europe. Great factories, subsidized by royal patronage, were established on the continent and rapidly rose to a place of prominence that resulted in both clear-cut and subtle influences on the English porcelain industry which began in the

4. Wolf Mankowitz, *Wedgwood* (B. T. Batsford Ltd, London 1953), p.33.

1740s. Yellow grounds were introduced at Meissen as early as the 1720s. Evidently, yellow was especially admired by Augustus the Strong, Meissen's patron. Subsequently, yellow grounds were employed, to a limited extent, by a number of major continental porcelain factories including Sèvres, Nymphenburg, Frankenthal, and Copenhagen. Some English porcelain, most probably influenced by continental examples, was also made with yellow grounds. Early pieces of Chelsea and Bow sometimes had yellow grounds, and Worcester and Derby both produced fine dinner services and individual pieces in yellow, often with white reserves containing fruit or flower painting. These ground colours were, of course, applied over the glaze and then re-fired.[5] The difficulty in ascribing sources for the use of ground colours is confirmed by the comments of H. Rissick Marshall in *Coloured Worcester Porcelain*:

> Worcester is justly famous for its use of ground colours, especially for its scale blue; it is therefore of interest to speculate upon the origin and development of these ground colours. However, in the entire absence of any factory records or other contemporary evidence, it must be insisted upon that any views put forward must necessarily be speculative and are unlikely to be either proved or disproved.[6]

Some observations on terminology are perhaps in order. The designation 'yellow-glazed earthenware' has been adopted, despite the somewhat cumbersome length, for two reasons. First, this term is descriptive and unambiguous. Second, a few surviving contemporary sources refer to 'yellow-glaze'. For example, this terminology was used by the Leeds Pottery (figure 1), and it seems reasonable that such usage was accepted.[7] Of course, any interpretation of contemporary references must be made with caution. The mere inclusion of the word 'yellow' cannot lead to the assumption that the yellow-glazed earthenware dealt with in this book is being described. The *Leeds Mercury* of 21 June 1774 advertised:

A NEW POTTERY
This is to inform the public that Samuel Shaw of Rothwell, potter (late from Staffordshire), makes and sells all sorts of cream colour, red, yellow, and painted wares, at his new pottery in Rothwell, where tradesmen and others may depend on being served at the very lowest prices, wholesale and retail.[8]

The reference to 'yellow . . . wares' is not clear, but when the term 'yellow wares' has been used in association with potteries such as Leeds, from which

5. Ground colours, including yellow, on eighteenth- and early nineteenth-century English porcelains are discussed in Stanley W. Fisher, *The Decoration of English Porcelain* (Derek Verschoyle, London 1954), Chapter 6.
6. H. Rissick Marshall, *Coloured Worcester Porcelain of the First Period* (The Ceramic Book Company, Newport, Mon. 1954), p.68.
7. *Leeds Price Book*, unpublished manuscript, Leeds Public Library.
8. Joseph R. & Frank Kidson, *Historical Notices of the Leeds Old Pottery* (J. R. Kidson, Leeds 1892), p.117.

marked pieces survive, it seems reasonable to consider 'yellow ware' as possibly synonymous with yellow-glazed earthenware.

Only a few recipes for the yellow glazes appear to have survived. The ingredients, in varying proportions, were litharge (lead monoxide), tin ash, sometimes lead ash, and antimony which gave the yellow colouring. Lawrence Harrison of Liverpool, as early as 1767, possessed a recipe calling for 9 parts litharge, 6 parts antimony, and 3 parts lead and tin ashes.[9] It is possible that this glaze was more closely related to Wedgwood's early yellow glaze. In the first quarter of the nineteenth century the Herculaneum Pottery in Liverpool possessed recipes for at least eight different yellow glazes.[10] One of these was called 'Delft Yellow' and another 'Lemmon'. The recipes for the Herculaneum

9. E. Stanley Price, *John Sadler, a Liverpool Pottery Printer* (published by the author, West Kirby, Cheshire 1948), p.89.
10. Manuscript records of Joseph and Benjamin Tompkinson, Herculaneum Managers. Collection of City of Liverpool Museum. Also see Alan Smith, *The Herculaneum Pottery* (Barrie & Jenkins Ltd, London 1970), pp.121-31.

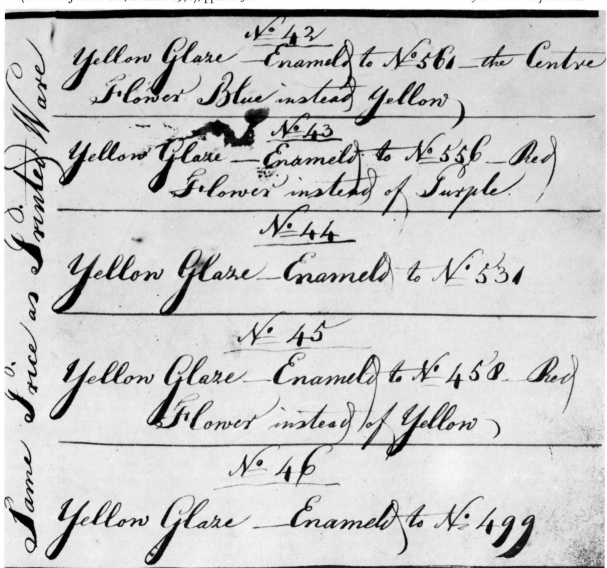

1. Extract from the *Leeds Pattern Book for Enamelled Teawares*, 1819. *Courtesy of the Leeds City Libraries*

glazes are given in Appendix A. Yellow was also included in the palette of the underglaze-decorated earthenwares of the so-called 'Prattware' type being produced in quantity during the first years of the nineteenth century. The recipes for underglaze yellow approximated those used to produce an overall yellow glaze. For example, the underglaze yellow employed by Thomas Lakin was made up of 4 parts litharge, 3 parts antimony and 10 parts tin oxide.[11]

The element chrome was discovered in the late eighteenth century and its qualities were investigated by eminent chemists such as Vauquelin and Klaproth.[12] Its colouring properties were understood quickly (hence its name), but the new element was not used immediately for glazes. By the 1830s (and perhaps earlier), chrome was introduced as a yellow colouring agent. This development was noted by Simeon Shaw in a technical work published in 1837, nearly a decade after the appearance of his controversial *History of the Staffordshire Potteries*.[13] At times, the nineteenth-century recipes are unclear as to whether antimony or chrome was to be used, merely specifying 'yellow calyx'.[14] It appears probable that most, if not all, of the yellow-glazed wares discussed in this book were coloured with antimony rather than chrome.

It is possible that the relatively small production of yellow-glazed earthenware resulted from difficulties in the glazing process. Though normally the preparation of glazes and the application by dipping were routine procedures,[15] the problem of obtaining consistency in yellow-glazed wares may have been more complex, and the even application of the glaze perhaps presented the most formidable obstacles.[16] Antimony, in particular, raises many problems for the potter, one of the worst being its tendency to produce blistering.

Today, many collectors and dealers use the term 'canary' or 'canary lustre'. This widely-accepted usage is somewhat unsatisfactory, since 'canary' really does not describe the colour involved. A cursory examination of any reasonably large group of yellow-glazed wares will show that the colour of individual pieces varies from pale yellow to deep yellow. Further, the term 'canary yellow' seems to be of fairly recent origin and there is little reason to perpetuate this usage.[17]

11. Taken from Section 3, Process 52 of *The Valuable Receipts of the Late Mr Thomas Lakin, Leeds* (printed for Mrs Lakin by Edward Baines, 1824). Victoria and Albert Museum Library.
12. James R. Partington, *A History of Chemistry* (Macmillan & Co. Ltd, London 1962), Vol.3, pp.553 and 658.
13. Simeon Shaw, *The Chemistry of the Several Natural and Artificial Heterogeneous Compounds Used in Manufacturing Porcelain, Glass and Pottery* (W. Lewis & Son, London 1837), p.518.
14. 'Calyx' was a vernacular synonym for 'oxide'. See the 'receipt for yellow' published in William Evens, *Art and History of the Potting Business* (Shelton 1846). Victoria and Albert Museum Library.
15. For example, see the description of glaze preparation and dipping in Evens, *ibid*, pp.44-5.
16. Comments on possible problems in glazing as relating to the limited production of yellow-glazed wares were received from Mr Arnold Mountford, Director, City Museum and Art Gallery, Stoke-on-Trent.
17. The earliest printed reference the author has found appears in W. Bosanko, *Collecting Old Lustre Ware* (William Heinemann Ltd, London 1916), pp.39-40, 'The canary ground is generally associated with nice work . . .'. By the 1930s the term was in common use. For example, see Stanley H. Lowndes Collection Auction Catalog, Anderson Galleries Inc., New York, 29 April-4 May 1935, item no.966, described as a 'Canary Yellow and Silver Lustre Pitcher'.

I. Leaf dish with silver lustre decoration. Possibly Leeds Pottery. c. 1810. 6¾ inches long.

II. Jug with silver resist lustre decoration. c. 1810-20. 7 inches high. Two-handled cup with silver resist lustre decoration. c. 1810-20. 5 inches high.

III. Coffee pot decorated with flowers in black enamel. c. 1810. $10\frac{3}{4}$ inches high.

IV. Jug painted with blue, red and green sprigs. c. 1820. 5 inches high. Teapot painted with pink roses. c. 1810-20. 6 inches high.

V. Plate with pierced rim and painted with iron-red stylized chrysanthemum outlined in silver lustre. c. 1815. Diameter 8 inches.

VI. Plate with gadrooned relief border and overall leaf and berry design painted in red, purple and green. c. 1820. Diameter 10 inches.

CHAPTER TWO

Lustre decoration

Yellow-glazed earthenwares were made in many parts of England roughly between 1785 and 1835. The body composition of these wares was similar to the creamwares and pearlwares of this period. Some yellow-glazed earthenwares received no additional decoration, but these were comparatively rare. Most of the undecorated pieces were figures. Moulded or engine-turned decoration was occasionally used without further overglaze painting or printing (figure 2). However, the great majority of yellow-glazed wares were given three basic types of decoration: lustre painting, enamel painting, or transfer-printing. These decorative techniques were not mutually exclusive. Frequently two, and sometimes all three types of decoration were applied to the same piece.

Accelerated technological advances in British ceramic production during the second half of the eighteenth century were accompanied by a proliferation of decorative techniques. A comparatively late arrival in the enlarged repertoire of ceramic decorations was the lustring process. Lustre painting had been introduced in the Middle East perhaps as early as the ninth century A.D., later spreading to Spain and Italy. Most standard ceramic histories place the commercial beginnings of lustre painting in England about 1800, though there is substantial evidence tending to prove that the production of lustre-decorated earthenwares pre-dated the turn of the century.[1] Noteworthy in this respect is a handsome silver resist jug (dated 1791) in the collections of the Henry Francis du Pont Winterthur Museum.[2]

1. William D. John and Warren Baker, *Old English Lustre Pottery* (R. H. Johns Ltd, Newport, Mon. 1951), p.12, note two silver lustre pieces dated 1792 and 1794. In this book, which presently is the standard reference work on the subject, the probable earliest dates for commercial production of English lustre wares are given (p.17) as follows: silver lustre c. 1800-05, gold lustre c. 1800-05, pink lustre c. 1805-15.

2. This important Winterthur piece indicates that the dating of the introduction of the various types of lustre decoration should probably be revised. Mr Robert Charleston, Keeper of Ceramics at the Victoria and Albert Museum, is currently researching this aspect of lustre decoration.

VII. Tea service painted in red and green with the 'single rose' design. c. 1820. Teapot $7\frac{1}{4}$ inches high.

VIII. Jug decorated with a songbird and flowers painted in black, red, blue and green. c. 1820. $5\frac{1}{2}$ inches high.

The application of metallic oxides which, after firing, produced a copper, gold, pink or silver metallic glaze soon proved technically feasible and commercially successful. The use of lustre on yellow-glazed wares was probably inevitable. It would appear that the marriage of silver lustre and the yellow glaze, from an aesthetic point of view, was a happy one. Indeed, though any such judgement is subjective, one might compare lustred creamwares with lustred yellow-glazed wares in order to ascertain the stronger visual impact of the latter. Continuing to consider the aesthetics involved, to most eyes silver lustre presents an especially suitable combination with the yellow ground. Silver was nearly always the colour selected, though a few pieces with copper lustre decoration (figure 3) may be encountered. The reason for this, most probably, is that the combination of copper and yellow simply appeared less pleasing to the early nineteenth-century eye, just as it does to the twentieth-century eye.

Rudimentary lustre decoration on yellow-glazed wares occurs as simple border lines. Often lustre rim lines were used in conjunction with transfer-printed decoration. Some yellow-glazed wares were hand-painted with silver lustre. The degree of such work ranged from hand-tipped lustre details to full-scale painted lustre decoration as seen in the leaf dish in plate I which is entirely covered with silver lustre, with the exception of oval reserves which allow the contrasting yellow to show through.

Like other industries, the potteries sought labour-saving techniques. The deliberate, slow process of hand-painting was expensive and subject to the difficulties encountered in employing and retaining competent decorators. Insofar as the application of lustre was concerned, stencilling was adopted as a time- and labour-saving technique.[3] Stencilled pieces can be readily distinguished by the mechanical nature of the lustre painting, as opposed to

2. Leaf dish, 1800-05. 5¾ inches long. Spill vase with engine-turned decoration. 5 inches high.

3. For a brief explanation of the stencil process, see John and Baker, p.23.

3. Flower pot with stand, decorated with a house pattern and copper lustre rims. c. 1815-30. 4 inches high.

4. Two jugs and a mug decorated with a scrolled staff and leaf motif. The lustre designs on the bodies are stencilled, while the foliate borders are resist decorated. c. 1810-20. Larger jug 6 inches high.

the rather freely conceived hand-painted designs. Further, when stencilling was used, the major design elements, i.e. birds, foliate motifs, etc., were in lustre against the yellow ground which was protected from the lustre. One of the most common stencil decorations consisted of alternating leaves and scrolled staffs (figure 4). Jugs stencilled with this design are not rare, but mugs and small pitchers are found far less frequently. A number of pieces with this particular design are of additional interest since they combine enamel painting, resist and stencilled lustre decoration, a feature not encountered by the author in any other yellow-glazed pieces.

Perhaps the finest examples of lustre decoration were painted in a manner that was essentially the reverse of the stencil technique. This was the so-called resist method, in which the chosen design was painted on with a special wax-like adhesive formula. The piece was then covered with silver lustre and dried. The parts painted with the adhesive 'resisted' the lustre, which only became fixed to the areas not treated. The resist was then removed and the piece fired, leaving the design in yellow standing out against the background of the lustred surfaces.[4] At times resist decoration on yellow-glazed pieces was both elaborate and detailed, the process allowing for meticulous drawing as well as airy, free-hand improvisation. Some of these characteristics can be seen in the jug resist decorated with exotic birds and flowers and in the two-handled loving cup decorated with elaborate foliate patterns in plate II.

4. *Ibid.,* p.23, for a more detailed explanation of the resist process.

CHAPTER THREE

Enamel decoration

Perhaps the most widespread decorative technique used on porcelains and the finer earthenwares made in eighteenth-century Europe consisted of painting in enamel colours over the glaze. These colours were fired, fixing the painted decoration to the glaze. The term 'enamel colours' is a rather loose one which conveniently encompasses the many overglaze colour recipes (often kept secret) used by china painters of the day. William B. Honey defined enamel colours as '... vitreous (glassy) colours fusing at a low temperature'.[1] In England during the period under consideration (c. 1780–1835) the alternative of cheaper and faster transfer-printing displaced some china painters, but vast amounts of porcelain and earthenware were still hand-painted.[2] In general, the finest enamel decoration was reserved for the elegant porcelains of the day, while the more commonplace earthenwares received relatively modest and less sophisticated painting. The yellow-glazed earthenwares fall within this latter category. Conceding this broadly-drawn distinction between enamel painting on porcelain and the humbler earthenwares, even the most perfunctory examination of enamel painting on the yellow-glazed wares reveals a surprising range, both in subject matter and in technique.

As with lustre-decorated pieces, the enamel wares also, at times, received a practically irreducible minimum of decoration. This restraint often produced satisfying results, the strong yellow ground requiring little embellishment. The coffee pot in plate III, with its sparse scattering of morning glories on a

1. William B. Honey, *European Ceramic Art* (Faber and Faber Ltd, London 1952), p.178. For a more detailed discussion of enamel painting, see Fisher, pp.1-5.
2. In a letter dated 12 September 1776 to his partner Thomas Bentley, Josiah Wedgwood commented that pieces decorated with coats of arms would have to be printed, at least in outline, in order to compete in the market. See Ann Finer and George Savage, eds., *The Selected Letters of Josiah Wedgwood* (Cory, Adams & Mackay Ltd, London 1965; The Born and Hawes Publishing Co., New York 1965), pp.197-8.

strong yellow ground, presents a delicate contrast in black and yellow. The specimen vase in figure 5, painted in black enamel with two women in an octagonal frame, again utilizes a single enamel colour against the yellow ground. This piece is of additional interest in that the design was probably taken from a contemporary print.

Flower painting was the most popular form of enamel decoration, and in quality and degree of complexity it ranged from extremely simple to elaborate. The great majority of flower-decorated pieces were painted in a stylized rather than naturalistic manner. This, of course, contrasted with much of the fine flower painting on eighteenth- and early nineteenth-century English porcelains which, frequently derived from Asiatic or continental European porcelains, was usually naturalistic and often drawn with precise botanical detail.[3] The

3. See Fisher, pp.57-70.

5. Specimen vase painted in black with a scene of two women in conversation. c. 1815-20. 8 inches high.

yellow-glazed earthenwares were painted with floral designs that, generally, were only vaguely representational. The treatment was sometimes delicate and at other times exuberant, tending towards the rather naive depiction found in other types of less elegant English ceramics of the period. The teapot and jug in plate IV demonstrate this: the octagonal teapot is painted with restraint, its rather sketchy pink roses indicating a pronounced feeling for space; the jug, on the other hand, repetitively painted with three rows of sprigs, attempts to solve the problem of space with uninspired duplication. The pierced plate in plate V, its centre covered entirely with a stylized chrysanthemum painted in yellow and iron-red and outlined in silver lustre, has a far greater exuberance than the jug with its rather cramped decoration. Indeed, exuberance and vitality seem to be hall-marks of much of the flower painting on yellow-glazed wares. It should be admitted, however, that many of these floral decorations display a lack of finesse. These factors, which often appeal to twentieth-century collectors as 'primitive', very probably resulted from economic and artistic limitations, rather than from aesthetic preference.

A favourite form of decoration seems to have been to cover large areas of a piece with these vigorous, somewhat stereotyped designs, the designs themselves being executed mainly in iron-reds and greens, with other colours used for details. The freely-drawn leaf and berry design on the plate in plate VI is representative. Other closely related patterns depict stylized tulips, primroses, roses (single and double), carnations, strawberries, and some hybrids that defy any precise botanical attribution. These patterns were most often used on tea services and plates of various sizes. None of the flower-decorated wares is marked, so the factories producing them or even the areas from which they came are, with few exceptions, unknown.

There are several aspects of these wares found in other English ceramics of roughly the same period. Some analogy can be drawn with the so-called 'king's rose' and 'queen's rose' patterns found on cream-coloured earthenwares of the late eighteenth and early nineteenth centuries. Further, the so-called 'Gaudy-Dutch' and 'Gaudy-Welsh' foliate decorations of the first half of the nineteenth century bear a superficial resemblance to the floral designs on the yellow-glazed wares. This resemblance is due to prevailing popular taste rather than to direct influence of one type upon the other.

Within this general group of floral-decorated yellow-glazed wares, the tea service in plate VII is especially outstanding. The vibrancy and vigorous execution of the design become apparent when comparison is made with other wares of this type. Also, though a number of single pieces or incomplete services with this general decoration (single or double rose) are known, possibly this is the only complete tea service with a floral decoration in existence. Another point to be mentioned is that the particular type of foliate decoration used on this tea service seems to be found only on yellow-glazed pieces. Perhaps it was thought unsuitable for the more abundant cream-coloured wares and pearlwares.

Though flower painting was the predominant type of enamel decoration on the yellow-glazed wares, there were a number of other decorative themes.

6. Jug painted with a rural
landscape in black. c. 1815-
25. $4\frac{1}{2}$ inches high.

7. Jug with relief decoration
of two pointers, painted in
brown, iron-red and green.
c. 1815-20. 6 inches high.

IX. Mug painted with a
peafowl in black, blue,
iron-red and green.
c. 1815-25. $2\frac{7}{8}$ inches high.

X. Jug with a moulded
diamond pattern painted
with a geometric pattern
in red and green, and with
silver lustre. c. 1820.
$5\frac{1}{2}$ inches high.

XI. Three satyr jugs
painted in enamel colours.
c. 1810-15. Jug on the left
5 inches high.

XII. Casters and a salt.
One caster is painted with
black, red and green dots;
the salt has an overall
sponged iron-red and green
decoration, and the second
caster is painted with
broad green sponged stripes.
All c. 1810-20. Sponged
caster $4\frac{1}{4}$ inches high.

XIII. Bowl with banded
and trailed decoration in
black, blue, grey and white.
c. 1825-35. Diameter 5
inches.

XIV. Jug printed with a
spaniel and two grouse;
the border is silver resist.
c. 1815-20. 6 inches high.

XV. Jug decorated with silver resist. In a circular yellow reserve is a black transfer-print based on the Cribb-Molineaux bouts of 1810-11, possibly after a Cruikshank or Rowlandson print. c. 1815. 6 inches high.

XVI. Jug printed with an equestrian portrait of Wellington at Salamanca. The print is overpainted with enamel colours. Probably made at the Glamorgan Pottery, Swansea. c. 1815. 6 inches high.

8. Plate with stylized tulip design and masonic emblems in relief, painted in iron-red and green. c. 1820-30. Diameter 8 inches.

Pastoral landscapes were sometimes used; usually these were little more than sketchily painted rural scenes, but some were carefully delineated, often in black enamels which contrasted well with the yellow ground, as in the jug in figure 6. Enamel-painted pieces decorated with animals or birds (plate VIII) are rarely encountered. The yellow-glazed mug in plate IX, painted in colours with a peafowl, is noteworthy because this bird, a common motif in the decoration of European pottery and porcelain, and drawn in the same sketchy manner, is also often found in a class of nineteenth-century earthenwares with various coloured grounds that were sponge decorated. These pieces, known in America as 'spatterware', were produced in Staffordshire for export, especially to Pennsylvania where the Germans found them very attractive.

Geometric patterns are another variant in enamelled decorations on yellow-glazed wares. The diamond-patterned jug in plate X, enamelled in strong red and green, is an example of this. Here it should be noted that enamel painting was used to emphasize and enhance a diamond-relief decoration. The combination of moulded pattern and enamel painting was also used in mask or satyr jugs (plate XI), which might be considered a special sub-category. During the late eighteenth and early nineteenth centuries grotesque mask jugs depicting leering satyrs (or perhaps Bacchus) were very popular in Europe. Silver jugs in this genre provided prototypes for porcelain manufacturers, and examples can be found in Chinese export porcelain as well as in English earthenwares and porcelains.[4] Many satyr jugs were produced in pearlware and these have survived in fairly large numbers. Again, the few surviving yellow-glazed, enamel-decorated satyr jugs indicate a limited production. In a similar vein, pearlware jugs with relief-decorated hunting scenes over-painted with enamel colours were common. Yellow-glazed ones (figure 7) were also produced. Other examples of enamel-painted, relief-moulded, yellow-glazed wares included plates decorated with raised masonic motifs (figure 8) and jugs with raised flower patterns (figure 9).

Sponged or powdered decoration is a further variant of over-glaze enamel painting, and is extremely rare in conjunction with yellow glaze. This long-established technique, frequently employed by English delftware manufacturers, was not especially favoured for the decoration of cream-coloured ware or pearlware. The caster and open salt in plate XII have sponged green enamel decoration.

When pearlware gained popularity during the first two decades of the nineteenth century, a broadly generalized decorative type of these modest ceramics was embellished with one or more horizontal, coloured bands. For convenience, these are termed 'banded wares', though frequently other painted decoration such as flowers or geometric motifs constituted a major

4. See John and Baker, pl.31c; F. Brayshaw Gilhespy, *Derby Porcelain* (MacGibbon and Kee Ltd, London 1961), pl.X.

9. Jug decorated with an overall flower relief pattern, painted in purple, iron-red, brown, green and silver lustre. c. 1820. $5\frac{1}{2}$ inches high.

part of the design. The bowl in plate XIII is an example of yellow-glazed banded ware. This piece also includes closely related design elements comprising various trailed and dabbed patterns, which are usually found in conjunction with banded decoration. The so-called 'Mocha' wares are near relatives of the pearlwares with trailed designs, but to date the author does not know of any 'Mocha' decoration on yellow-glazed earthenware. It should be noted, however, that the French potteries at Creil and Montreaux made some yellow-glazed wares with a 'Mocha'-type decoration.

CHAPTER FOUR

Transfer-printed decoration

The full impact of the discovery of the transfer-printing process in England, in the mid-eighteenth century, was not felt until a considerably later date. The final decades of the eighteenth century and the first two decades of the nineteenth century saw a swing to this cheap, fast, decorative process which revolutionized a substantial portion of England's ceramic industry.[1] As noted in Chapter II, the advent of transfer-printing extended the range of available decorative techniques. The makers of yellow-glazed wares, as might be expected, followed this general trend and much of their production was transfer-printed. As in the case of cream-coloured earthenware, the printing was nearly always done over the glaze. Most of the prints on yellow-glazed wares were in black, but red and brown were occasionally used.

Though transfer-printing represented an advanced technical development within the industry, the choice of subject matter for printed decoration generally remained catholic. The well-established European interest in landscape and topography was continued, indeed championed, by the potteries using transfer-printing. From an aesthetic point of view, the results were decidedly debatable. Commercially-printed landscapes seem to have been successful at the time. It might be added that this popularity continued throughout the nineteenth century. The landscapes printed on yellow-glazed wares (as in the case of enamel-painted pieces) were rather unexceptional scenes ranging from simple, stylized views to competently engraved and printed ones.

Scenes of country houses, often including sheep, cows and miscellaneous

1. English transfer-printing has, to date, been the subject of only one inclusive study, William Turner, *Transfer Printing on Enamels, Porcelain and Pottery* (Chapman and Hall Ltd, London 1907). The work of one of the pioneers of the art, Robert Hancock, is described in some detail in Cyril Cook, *The Life and Work of Robert Hancock* (Chapman and Hall Ltd, London 1948).

10. Jug printed in black with a scene of a country house. c. 1810-20. 6½ inches high.

rustics, were favoured. It must be admitted that many of these views of great houses were stereotyped, perhaps inspired by such work as the hand-painted landscapes enamelled on bone china services by John Cutts at Wedgwood, about 1813-16. The jug in figure 10 is representative of this genre. Ranging downwards from the great country houses, more modest farmhouses and farmyard scenes were also subjects for printed decoration.[2] Especially unusual is a jug (figure 11) with a shepherd and his flock printed in red on one side and with pigs in a farmyard printed in black on the reverse. The great majority of early nineteenth-century transfer-decorated earthenwares (yellow-glazed or cream-coloured) was printed in only a single colour: printing in different colours on the obverse and reverse was seldom done.

More romanticized landscapes also were favoured. Pastoral scenes of Watteau-type lovers, castles and ruins reflect a continuation of the eighteenth-century predilection for such themes. Somewhat more common was a scene of an *al fresco* tea party printed in red or black, descending, albeit remotely, from versions of a popular Worcester print by Robert Hancock, c. 1760.[3] Printed chinoiserie landscapes were rare in yellow-glazed wares.

Birds and animals provided appealing subjects. The small, footed bowl in figure 12 is printed in black with a goldfinch and a yellow bunting. These birds were copied from woodcuts by Thomas Bewick, first published in his *History of British Birds* (first edition, 1797). The lion printed in red on the mug

2. See Fisher, pl.86, p.173; Mankowitz, pp.138-9.
3. See Cook, items 104-6.

in figure 13 is also after a woodcut by Bewick, taken from *The Figures of Bewick's Quadrupeds* (first edition, 1790). These publications became prime source materials for copper plate engravers supplying the English earthenware manufacturers.[4] The bowl with the Bewick birds was probably made at the Cambrian Pottery, Swansea, and the mug also is possibly by the same maker.[5]

Allegorical and mythological prints were also used on yellow-glazed wares, but only to a limited extent, whereas complex and extensive decorations of these kinds were championed by Wedgwood. Wedgwood's market was mainly comprised of more sophisticated and well-to-do English people who would have been very interested in the neo-classical revival, but transfer-printed

4. Many of Bewick's woodcuts have been assembled by Blanche Aiker, ed., in *1800 Woodcuts by Thomas Bewick and His School* (Dover Publications, New York 1962). This volume is helpful in quick research for transfer-print sources.
5. See E. Morton Nance, *The Pottery and Porcelain of Swansea and Nantgarw* (B. T. Batsford Ltd, London 1942), p.102 and pl.XLVII H.

11. Jug printed in red with a rural scene. The reverse is printed in black with a different rural scene. Probably Sunderland Pottery. c. 1815-25. $4\frac{3}{4}$ inches high.

12. Footed bowl printed in black with a goldfinch copied from a woodcut by Thomas Bewick. Probably Cambrian Pottery, Swansea. c. 1815. Diameter 3¾ inches. *Gift to the Leon Collection from Mr and Mrs W. J. Grant-Davidson*

13. Mug printed in dark red with a lion after Thomas Bewick. c. 1810-20. 4 inches high.

earthenwares would have been sold mostly to the less affluent, middlebrow Englishmen to whom the glories of antiquity meant little. By far the most popular subjects for yellow-glazed wares were the symbolic figures of 'Faith', 'Hope' and 'Charity'—they were a favourite iconographic cliché in the early nineteenth century. The vase in figure 14, with the figure of 'Charity' printed in black, is probably exceptional, all the other yellow-glazed examples with these figures, known to the author, being jugs and mugs (figure 15). It was not uncommon for transfer-prints to be overpainted in enamel colours. Such is the case with the jug in figure 15 (left), with 'Faith' represented on the obverse side and 'Charity' on the reverse. Mythological decorations included

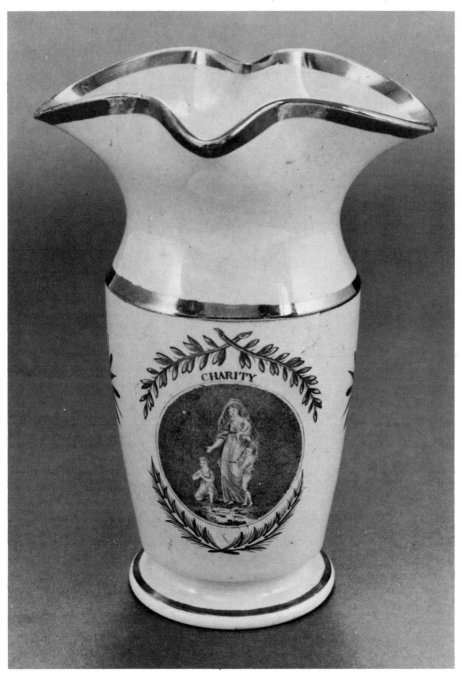

14. Vase printed in black with a figure of 'Charity'. c. 1815. 7 inches high.

Aurora in her chariot, assorted cupids and Bacchus types, and a few other scenes that appear to have vaguely classical origins.

Transfer-printed decorations depicting various sporting activities were often used for yellow-glazed wares. Here, most probably, was a less sophisticated area closer to the heart of the Englishman who might purchase yellow pieces or use them in local inns. Many of the more important English sporting activities were represented. Hunting was depicted in a number of transfer-printed views, but in scenes of simpler forms of hunting, such as shooting birds or rabbits, not of fox hunting. Scenes of the chase would have been reserved for fine porcelains, for example, Chinese export porcelain or Worcester. This again indicates the market for which yellow-glazed pieces were intended. The printed hunting scenes were varied and, as usual in the potteries, were probably copied from prints and book illustrations. A handsome example of this group is the jug in plate XIV; printed on one side is a pair of pointers and on the reverse a spaniel and two grouse. Other pieces with hunting motifs include views of bird shooting, various types of hunting dogs, rabbit hunters, and 'return from the hunt' scenes. A number of transfer-printed views on yellow-glazed wares include fishermen or fisherwomen, but the landscape rather than the sport of fishing receives the main emphasis.

Professional boxing became immensely popular in early nineteenth-century England, and a number of important matches were commemorated in transfer-printed earthenware. George Cruikshank and Thomas Rowlandson both drew boxing scenes from which prints were made. Two particularly famous matches between the champion Tom Cribb and Tom Molineaux, an American Negro challenger, inspired the printed decoration on the jug in plate XV.[6]

15. Two jugs and a mug printed in black with 'Faith', 'Hope', and 'Charity'. c. 1815. The print on the jug on the left is overpainted with enamel colours. Mug 4½ inches high.

6. See Paul Magriel, 'Pugilism in English Pottery', *Antiques* (January 1948), pp.58-9. Magriel attributes a silver-resist jug with the Cribb-Molineaux print to Brislington, but does not give the reason for this attribution. A contrary view is expressed in John and Baker, pp.25-8, who assert that lustre-decorated wares were not made at Brislington.

16. Jug printed in black with a scene of the sport of 'single stick'. c. 1810-20. 6 inches high.

Though not an exact copy, it seems probable that the engraving for this print was based on similar drawings by Cruikshank and Rowlandson. Another combative sport, single-stick fighting, also was depicted, as in the jug in figure 16.

A particular area of interest to the decorators of transfer-printed yellow-glazed wares encompassed politics and major or minor historical events. Here again, the cream-coloured printed wares were given more varied political and historical subjects, but many of the more interesting prints also can be found on yellow-glazed wares. Sir Francis Burdett, the Whig who was imprisoned in the Tower of London, was especially popular as a political subject (figure 17). Whether the many pieces decorated with Burdett's portrait were merely commemorative or whether they were actually used as campaign material poses a particularly interesting question. The English ceramic historian Bevis Hillier is inclined to the latter point of view, stating that:

The eighteenth century electioneering pottery, painted with inscriptions such as 'Sir Francis Burdett for Ever', was bought in quantity by candidates and distributed free to the inn keepers of their constituencies.[7]

7. Bevis Hillier (ed. Hugh Honour), *The Social History of the Decorative Arts—Pottery and Porcelain 1700-1914* (Weidenfeld & Nicolson Ltd, London and Meredith Press, New York 1968) p.121.

17. Jug printed in black with a portrait of Francis Burdett. J. Phillips & Co., Sunderland. Under the portrait is printed 'Sunderland Potery'. c. 1812. 5 inches high.

If this was a common practice, it would seem that more pieces of this so-called 'electioneering pottery', with many different political portaits, would have survived. However, the portraits of only a few early nineteenth-century politicians are found on printed wares of the period. The rare yellow jug in figure 18 is printed with a portait entitled 'Henry Hunt, Esq.'. Hunt (1773–1835) was, like Burdett, a popular leader of the reform movement who was specially noted for having presided at the historic meeting on 16 August 1819 at St Peter's Fields, Manchester, which culminated in the so-called Peterloo Massacre. In fact, the portrait on this jug appears not to be of Hunt, but rather of the American naval hero Captain James Lawrence. During the period immediately following the conclusion of the War of 1812, Lawrence was a popular subject on printed cream-coloured wares made for the American trade. The printers for the various Staffordshire potteries were, at times, not too particular as to which portrait was used, especially when time was short for placing a new popular hero on the market. It seems probable that after the Peterloo Massacre, no print or portrait of Henry Hunt being readily available, the printers of this particular jug resorted to using the Lawrence engraving.[8]

One enamel-decorated and printed yellow-glazed jug (figure 19) commemorates a small political victory. This piece, probably made at the Cambrian Pottery, Swansea, bears the arms of Pembroke and also various inscriptions

8. For an illustration of one of the Lawrence jugs with the identical portrait as used for Henry Hunt, Esq., see Ellouise Baker Larsen, *American Historical Views on Staffordshire China* (Doubleday & Company, Inc., Garden City, N.Y. 1950), p.272, no.770.

34

18. Jug printed with a portrait titled 'Henry Hunt Esq'. This is identical to the printed portraits of the American naval captain James Lawrence, used on commemorative pieces made at the time of the War of 1812. c. 1820. $3\frac{5}{8}$ inches high.

19. Jug printed with the Arms of Pembroke. The border is silver resist. Cambrian Pottery, Swansea. c. 1812. $4\frac{1}{2}$ inches high.

which triumphantly detail the election of Sir John Owen to Parliament in 1812, and announce that Owen has also been created Baronet in the same year.[9]

International politics and military events gave rise to many transfer-printed decorations for yellow-glazed wares. These included Napoleonic War cartoons, celebrations of Wellington's victories during the Peninsula campaign (plate XVI) and a portrait of England's ally, Czar Alexander of Russia. This last is on a jug which has a print of masonic emblems on the reverse; the importance of the Masons in early nineteenth-century English (and American) society is attested by the many printed masonic decorations on the cream-coloured and yellow-glazed earthenwares of the time.

Though landscapes, sporting views and political scenes represent the main decorative themes on printed yellow wares, there were many other individual decorations covering a very wide range of subjects. Perhaps the most common were the various prints derived from the drawings of Adam Buck (1775–1833), a portrait artist of modest talent. He was a member of the Royal Academy, where he exhibited over the years, and he obtained some success in London. The rather cloying domestic scenes of ladies and children dressed in the empire fashion were recurring themes in Buck's drawings. Such topics evidently had great appeal at the time, and printed ceramics from a number of potteries were decorated with versions of Buck's drawings. One of the most popular was the print of the empire-gowned lady at the piano, with two children listening, depicted on the tea service in figure 20.[10] Many pieces from services such as this were made at the Ouseburn Pottery operated by Robert Maling after 1817. Other pieces with Buck prints are impressed 'Sewell', the name of the proprietor of the St Anthony's Pottery, Newcastle-upon-Tyne (1804–c. 1828). Scenes of tea parties, children playing and ladies reclining on récamier couches were also used.

20. Tea service printed in black with a view of a lady and two children at the piano, after Adam Buck. Probably Robert Maling's Ouseburn Pottery. c. 1820. Teapot 4 inches high.

9. Owen represented the Welsh county of Pembroke for most of the period 1812-41. See Nance, pp.105-6, pls.L E and LI A.
10. A copper plate used for transfer-printing and engraved with a scene of a lady at the piano is in the collections of the Laing Art Gallery and Museum, Newcastle-upon-Tyne. This plate was possibly engraved by Adam Buck. It is unsigned, but was in the possession of the Maling family and has been traditionally attributed to Buck. (Source of this information, B. Collingwood Stevenson, Director, Laing Art Gallery and Museum.)

21. Two mugs transfer
printed in black with 'Beer'
and 'Porter'. c. 1810-25.
'Porter' mug $3\frac{1}{4}$ inches
high.

22. Mug printed in black
with a scene from
Shakespeare's *Henry IV*,
Part 3. c. 1820. $2\frac{1}{2}$ inches
high.

23. Jug printed in black with a portrait of Ann Moore. c. 1815. 5¾ inches high.

A miscellany of labels, mottoes, and quotations are found on transfer-printed yellow-glazed wares, ranging from 'Beer' and 'Porter' (figure 21), 'The Farmers Arms', and 'Peace and Roast Beef to the Friends of Liberty' to Shakespeare's 'Oh pity, pity gentle heaven' (figure 22). Nautical views, predictably, were sometimes resorted to, and these included scenes of stereotyped sailing vessels and 'box the compass' prints, both types being common in the cream-coloured wares of the period.

An unusual transfer print is the one depicting Ann Moore (figure 23). Ann Moore carried off a delightful hoax in the early nineteenth century, claiming (as the legend on the jug diligently explains) to have taken neither food nor drink for nine years. It is possible that these yellow-glazed jugs and mugs were sold as souvenir items to those who had already been lured into paying a fee for the privilege of viewing this abstemious lady.

A wide variety of interesting decorative motifs were used for transfer-prints on yellow-glazed wares, and taken together they provide social historians as well as ceramic historians with a wealth of information about contemporary events and taste.

XVII. Plate with relief decoration of leaves and grapes, painted in black, brown, red and green. c. 1820. Diameter $8\frac{3}{8}$ inches.

XVIII. Leaf dish painted brown, red and green. Probably Leeds Pottery. c. 1790. $5\frac{3}{4}$ inches long.

XIX. Presentation mug painted with a strawberry design in red, green and silver lustre. c. 1810-15. 6 inches high.

XX. Beaker, dated 1804, painted in brown, iron-red, orange and green. 3 inches high.

XXI. Flask decorated with a relief portrait of a pipe smoker and painted in enamel colours. c. 1810-20. 7¾ inches high.

XXII. Two wall plaques, with painted details in red, green and silver lustre. c. 1810. Both plaques 8 inches high. *right* Possibly Leeds Pottery.

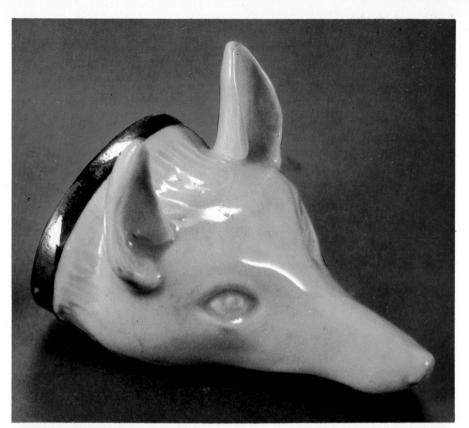

XXIII. Stirrup cup with
silver lustre rim. c. 1810.
4¾ inches long.

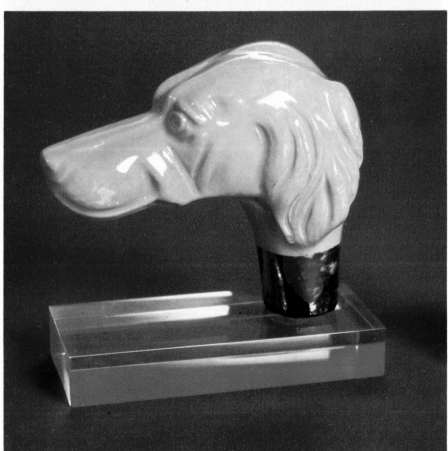

XXIV. Cane handle with a
silver lustre band at the
base. c. 1810. 2½ inches high.

CHAPTER FIVE

Forms

Yellow-glazed eathenware was produced in nearly all the forms in which the more common creamware and pearlware are found. There appears to have been one major exception: complete yellow-glazed dinner services were probably never made. Large serving platters and tureens are unknown to the author and smaller serving dishes are rare. In considering the various elements of the dinner services of the period, the evidence suggests that yellow-glazed wares were used as accessories for the dinner table, but that they made up entire services for the tea table.

Plates were made in yellow glaze in various sizes. The smallest of these are cup plates, averaging $3-3\frac{1}{2}$ inches in diameter, and used with tea and coffee cups. Slightly larger in size are the so-called 'cockle' plates. Larger plates 6–9 inches in diameter are not uncommon. These were probably used for biscuits and sandwiches at tea time, rather than on the dinner table. Their decoration includes transfer-printing, enamel overglaze painting, and lustre. Most of the surviving plates have unexceptional decoration, but a few are noteworthy. One such (plate XVII) is relief-decorated with grapes and leaves and over-painted in brown, several shades of red, black and green. Leaf dishes appear particularly successful in yellow glaze. The delicate leaf dish in plate XVIII, overpainted in brown, red and green, is probably a product of the Leeds Pottery. A similar creamware dish in the Schreiber Collection at the Victoria and Albert Museum has been attributed to Leeds and dated about 1790.[1]

Though yellow-glazed tea services seem to have been made in quantity, few have survived intact. The tea service in plate VII, decorated with stylized leaves and flowers in strong red and green, is representative of a large group of

1. Bernard Rackham, *Catalogue of the Schreiber Collection* (Board of Education, London 1930), Vol.II, no.347.

yellow-glazed tea wares painted in this manner. Whether this distinctive design and palette were produced by one or several factories is unclear. Strangely-mannered foliate painting of this type seems to be found only in yellow-glazed tea wares. Creamwares decorated in these colours and with this design are presently unknown to the author. Child's tea wares (figure 24), small tea and coffee pots for single servings, and tiny cups and saucers for children's play (or perhaps for dolls' houses) were also made in yellow glaze. Within this category there are a number of pieces bearing factory marks.

Probably the commonest form found in yellow-glazed wares is the jug or pitcher. The advent of packaging in the food industry has now substantially curtailed the need for jugs on the table and in the kitchen, but in the early nineteenth century every liquid in a household required a container, hence the profusion of jugs and the variety of sizes. All the decorative techniques found in yellow-glazed wares were used in the jugs. Some very small examples were toys and the few existing very large examples were used possibly as interior shop signs. The sizes in between, in most cases, were designed for multiple household or tavern uses. The range in form and decoration for these jugs is extensive.[2]

Mugs form the next most numerous category. Again, they vary from large ones (about 7 inches high) to miniatures. Included in this group are children's mugs (figure 25) which must have been popular as gifts. Many are labelled with proper names, while others bear legends such as 'A present for a good boy'. Most are transfer-printed.

A number of yellow-glazed tablewares were obviously presentation pieces. Some were painted with a monogram, presumably of the owner, such as the

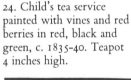

24. Child's tea service painted with vines and red berries in red, black and green, c. 1835-40. Teapot 4 inches high.

2. For other illustrations of yellow-glazed jugs, see John and Baker, colour illus.2, 31 and 62. The Burnap Collection in the Nelson Gallery-Atkins Museum, Kansas City, Missouri has a number of fine yellow-glazed jugs. See Ross E. Taggart, *The Frank P. and Harriet C. Burnap Collection of English Pottery* (Nelson Gallery-Atkins Museum, enlarged and rev. edn, Kansas City, Missouri 1967), pp.177-9.

25. A group of children's mugs. c. 1820-30. Average 2 inches high.

mug decorated with a stawberry motif and a monogram in plate XIX. A more unusual form is seen in the two-handled cup in plate XLI painted with the name 'Jonathan Hawksworth' and dated 1812 on the reverse. The small beaker in plate XX, dated 1804, is significant as this is the earliest dated piece of yellow-glaze ware known to the author at this time. Presentation pieces of this type were, of course, not uncommon in creamware.

In addition to the more usual forms that have been discussed, many other forms were produced. The list of tablewares found in yellow-glaze is quite extensive.

cup plates	jugs	beakers
cockle plates	mugs	two-handled cups
plates	punch bowls	butter tubs
soup plates	mustard pots	sweetmeat dishes
pickle dishes	egg cups	baskets and stands
leaf-shaped dishes	ladles	nut baskets and dishes
vegetable dishes	casters	compotes
tea and coffee services	salts	sauceboats
jardinières	small tureens	goblets
chocolate pots	cow creamers	
strawberry dishes and stands	strainers	

Though the majority of forms found in yellow-glazed earthenware are tablewares, pieces with a variety of other uses were also made.

Vases and flower holders were produced in a number of shapes and given printed, lustred or enamelled decoration. The urn-shaped vase in figure 26 with relief foliate bandings painted in black incorporates a decorative motif employed by several English manufacturers including Wedgwood, who used a similar vine and flower border in late eighteenth-century jasperwares.[3] Other forms of vases included specimen vases (figure 5) and graceful containers with fluted tops (figure 14). Some vases (or possibly pot pourris) were made with perforated holes intended to space individual stems. There were also flower pots and stands, made in a number of sizes and usually enamel-painted with red and green flowers and brown rim lines. Perhaps the product of one factory, these flower pots were probably made in large numbers since many have survived. Another type of vase made in yellow glaze, though intended for a different purpose, was the spill vase (figure 2).

Simple functional pieces were manufactured in yellow glaze to serve various household purposes. These include kitchen moulds for jelly or butter, flasks (figure 27 and plate XXI), quill holders, snuff or patch boxes, banks and wash bowls. Decorative plaques were also made in yellow glaze (plate XXII). The stirrup cup in the shape of a vixen's head in plate XXIII is the only yellow-glazed stirrup cup known to the author. Another rarity is a cane handle in the shape of a hound's head (plate XXIV). Though cane handles were frequently made of porcelain, few earthenware examples exist. The softer earthenware, it would seem, could not have been a suitable material for this purpose.

3. See Mankowitz, fig.103. For a Spode example, see Whiter, *Spode* (Barrie & Jenkins Ltd, London and Praeger Publishers, New York 1970), fig.150.

26. Vase with relief foliate decoration painted in black. c. 1800. $5\frac{1}{4}$ inches high.

27. Flask painted with flowers in black. c. 1800–25. 6 inches high.

28. Candleholder with silver lustre borders. c. 1815. 6 inches high.

29. Butter tub decorated with a leaf design in copper lustre and enamel colours. Probably Cambrian Pottery, Swansea. c. 1820. 5 inches high.

30. Ladle and egg cup decorated with silver lustre. c. 1810-15. Ladle $6\frac{7}{8}$ inches long, egg cup $3\frac{1}{8}$ inches high. Strainer. Probably Leeds. c. 1800-10. 3 inches long over handle.

Furniture supports dating from the early nineteenth century represent a little-known ceramic use. These supports were evidently made in sets of four, and their exact function is open to some conjecture. Probably they were used as stands for dresser mirrors or for other small pieces of furniture. The pair of supports in plate XXV are enamel-painted in black, purple, red and green, with details in silver lustre. The head is possibly that of Wellington.[4] Vessels for feeding infants (milkpots) were usually in all white pearlware, but a few yellow ones (plate XXVI) were made. Another utilitarian household object rarely found in yellow glaze is the candle-holder (figure 28).

Thus, the range of forms in which yellow-glazed wares are to be found is quite extensive. As has been shown, the forms are for the most part the same as those for creamwares and pearlwares. Considering the yellow-glazed wares on the basis of form alone, it would seem that they should not be categorized as an entirely separate type of English ceramics, but rather as a variety of creamware and pearlware.

4. For a furniture support from the same mould, but decorated overall with gold lustre, see John and Baker, illus.92A.

XXV. Furniture supports, possibly depicting Welling-ton, painted in black, purple, red, green and silver lustre. c. 1810-20. 4¼ inches high.

XXVI. Milkpot (feeding vessel for a baby). c. 1800-20. 4 inches high.

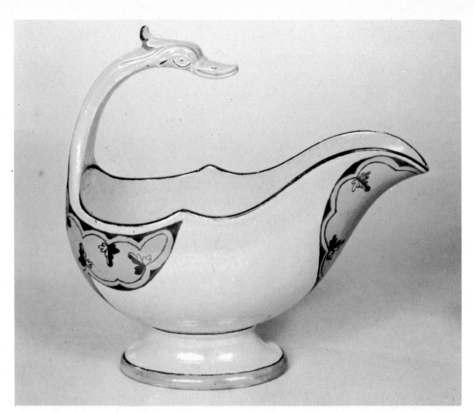

XXVII. Sauceboat painted in
black and green. c. 1800–20.
$6\frac{3}{4}$ inches long.

XXVIII. Coffee pot painted
in brown, red and green.
c. 1810–25. $11\frac{3}{4}$ inches high.
*The Greenwood Gift, the
National Museum of History
and Technology, Smith-
sonian Institution*

XXIX. Cow cream jug
with sponged decoration in
brown. c. 1800-10.
5 inches long.

XXX. Teapot with moulded
shell pattern painted with
green borders. Mark:
'WEDGWOOD' impressed.
c. 1785. 4 inches high.

XXXI. Chocolate pot and
cover painted in red and
green. Mark: 'WEDG-
WOOD' impressed.
c. 1790–1800. 5 inches high.

XXXII. Bowl with shell
border and lustre rim and
interior. Mark: 'WEDG-
WOOD' impressed.
c. 1790–1810. 2½ inches high.

XXXIII. Leaf dish edged in green. Mark: 'WEDG-WOOD' impressed. c. 1790-1800. 9 inches long.

XXXIV. Strawberry dish and stand. Mark: 'I SHORTHOSE' impressed. c. 1800. Dish $9\frac{1}{2}$ inches long.

XXXV. Jug with a diamond-quilted relief pattern painted with silver lustre. Probably Thomas Harley's pottery in Lane End. c. 1802–8. 12 inches high.

XXXVI. Two cup plates, painted in black, iron-red and green. Mark: 'HACK-WOOD' impressed. c. 1830. Diameter 3¼ inches.

XXXVII. Jug and cover painted with red and blue. Mark: 'BRAMELD' impressed. c. 1810–20. Height 5 inches.

XXXVIII. Pair of melon-shaped tureens with details painted in light green. Mark: 'LEEDS ★ POTTERY' impressed. c. 1785. 8 inches long, 5½ inches high.

XXXIX. Plate with
stencilled silver lustre
decoration. Probably Leeds.
c. 1810–20. Diameter $8\frac{1}{2}$
inches.

XL. Basket and stand
painted in brown, red and
green. Probably Leeds
c. 1800–10. Stand $8\frac{3}{4}$
inches long.

CHAPTER SIX

The manufacturers

The wide range in form, decoration, paste and glaze of yellow-glazed English earthenwares indicates that they were made by a considerable number of potteries during the period from about 1785 to about 1835. There was no stringent rule or prevailing custom about the use of factory marks and, as with other types of English ceramics of the period, some yellow-glazed wares were marked but most were not. The list of known marked pieces gives the names of a representative group of English manufacturers. This number can be augmented by other factories on the basis of stylistic attribution. Certainly, the making of yellow-glazed wares was not the province of just a few potteries, though in most instances production was limited. In considering the marked or attributed pieces of English yellow-glazed earthenware known at this time, it seems logical to present them within a geographical context, beginning with Staffordshire.

The firm of Josiah Wedgwood was one of England's major producers of creamwares and pearlwares and it does not seem surprising to find that Wedgwood made yellow-glazed wares. Yet until recent years Wedgwood collectors and scholars were, for the most part, unaware that Wedgwood produced earthenwares with an overall yellow glaze. Now, the number of known pieces of Wedgwood with this type of decoration would appear to put to rest the possibility that Wedgwood yellow-glazed wares were experimental pieces or anomalies. Though Josiah Wedgwood I had experimented with a yellow glaze at about the time of his partnership with Thomas Whieldon (1754-9) and had used a yellow lead glaze in his early moulded imitations of pineapples and melons, he probably did not turn to the manufacturing of overall yellow-glazed wares until after his partnership with Thomas Bentley had ended with the latter's death in 1780. Of the eleven marked Wedgwood pieces in the Leon

Collection, perhaps the earliest is a teapot (plate XXX) decorated with a moulded shell pattern at the upper rim of the pot and on the spout, with an interlaced twist handle and a flower finial on the lid. The moulded shell edges are outlined in green. This pot may be dated about 1785.[1] A small Wedgwood chocolate pot and cover (plate XXXI) decorated with borders in red and green probably dates about 1790–1800.[2] Another Wedgwood piece that possibly pre-dates the nineteenth century is the bowl in plate XXXII with a shell-moulded border surmounted by a silver lustre band.[3] Though, as previously pointed out, the prevailing view appears to be that silver lustre decoration did not come into common commercial use until after about 1805, it seems possible that this date should be put back, at least to the last decade of the eighteenth century[4]. A fourth Wedgwood piece may also be assigned a date about 1790–1800. This is an intricately shaped leaf dish outlined in green (plate XXXIII). A larger group of marked Wedgwood pieces date between about 1810 and 1830. These include a child's teapot and creamer (figure 31) made in a standard Wedgwood neo-classical shape. A few other pieces, of which a sauce tureen and cover provide an example (figure 32), are painted in enamel colours with

1. A Wedgwood creamware teapot with transfer-printed decoration and having the same form is in the Schreiber Collection in the Victoria and Albert Museum. This piece has been dated about 1770. See Bernard Rackham, *Catalogue of the Schreiber Collection,* Vol.II, no.353.
2. For a similar Wedgwood pot in creamware, see published papers of *The Ninth Wedgwood International Seminar, 1964* (The Wedgwood International Seminar, New York 1971), p.254.
3. Many pieces of creamware with this moulded border are illustrated in the extensive literature on Wedgwood. Most are dated about 1775. For example, see Mankowitz, fig.39.
4. See Chapter II, Note 2.

31. Child's creamer and teapot from a part tea service painted in black and green. Mark: 'WEDGWOOD' impressed. c. 1810-20. Teapot 5½ inches long.

32. Sauce tureen and cover painted with a strawberry pattern in red, brown, green and silver lustre. Possibly decorated outside the factory. Mark: 'WEDG-WOOD' impressed. c. 1810-20. 6 inches long.

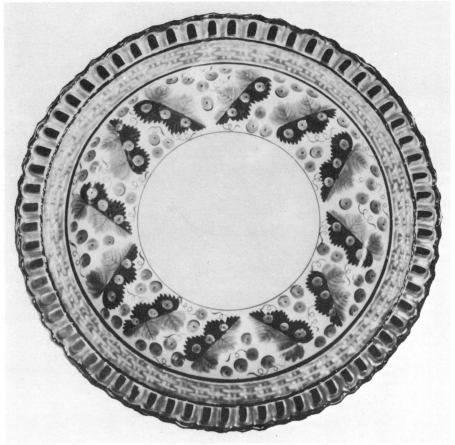

33. Plate painted with a leaf pattern in red-brown and green. Mark: 'Spode' impressed. c. 1805-10. Diameter 7½ inches.
Collection of Mr and Mrs Harry Epstein

geometric or foliate designs and with borders of silver lustre. The painting on these pieces is mediocre at best and has a primitive quality, raising the possibility that the overglaze decoration was done outside the factory.

One of Wedgwood's competitors was the firm established by Josiah Spode. In the first quarter of the nineteenth century, when Wedgwood and Spode were Staffordshire's premier factories, Spode too made at least some yellow-glazed earthenware. A rare, marked pair of Spode yellow-glazed, pierced-edge plates (figure 33) are in an American collection. Painted with a leaf pattern in red-brown and green, these plates date from about 1805–10.[5] Another Staffordshire pottery known for its versatility was Davenport, established in Longport about 1793. In the early nineteenth century an impressive variety of porcelains and earthenwares were made there, including some marked yellow-glazed earthenwares. The small oval tray from Davenport (figure 34), painted with a pastoral scene in black, dates from about 1820. Polychrome enamel decoration and transfer-printing were also used in the Davenport yellow-

34. Tray painted with a landscape in black. Mark: 'DAVENPORT' and anchor, impressed. c. 1820. 7¼ inches long.

5. For a creamware example with identical form and decoration, see Leonard Whiter, fig.132.

35. Cup plate decorated with a green floral design and silver lustre outlines. Mark: 'DAVENPORT' and anchor, impressed. c. 1820-30. Diameter 3¾ inches.

36. *right* Plate printed in red with a scene of a tower. Mark: 'ENOCH WOOD & SONS BURSLEM' impressed. c. 1820. Diameter 8⅝ inches. *left* Plate printed in black with a mythological scene of Aurora in her chariot. Diameter 10 inches.

glazed wares. The Davenport cup plate in figure 35 combines silver lustre with a simple floral design painted in green.

Spode and Wedgwood had succeeded in establishing themselves as producers of earthenwares of the most elegant sort, while at the same time manufacturing large amounts of more modest wares for home consumption and for export. Competing in this huge market for everyday-type earthenwares was another important Staffordshire firm, Enoch Wood & Sons (1818–46). With some possible exceptions this pottery did not aspire to the luxury trade, but produced a wide range of simpler wares. The marked plate in figure 36 printed in red with a pastoral scene dominated by a castle is important, not only in itself, but as a means of attribution. The distinctive relief border provides reasonable' grounds for assigning similar but unmarked transfer-printed yellow-glazed plates to this firm. As noted earlier in Chapter IV, one of the commonest transfer prints on yellow-glazed wares depicted an empire-gowned

37. Cup and saucer printed in black with a scene after Adam Buck. Mark: 'WOOD' impressed.
c. 1800–20. Cup $2\frac{1}{2}$ inches high, saucer diameter $5\frac{1}{4}$ inches.

38. Teapot printed in red. Mark: 'Shorthose & Co' in cursive red over the glaze. c. 1810. 3 inches high.

lady at the piano. Tea services with this printed decoration are usually attributed with good reason to the Ouseburn Pottery in Newcastle-upon-Tyne, operated by members of the Maling family. However, a slightly different version of this same scene may have been produced by Enoch Wood. A cup and saucer with the impressed mark 'WOOD' (figure 37) presents a problem. This impressed mark was used by Enoch Wood from about 1784 to 1792 and perhaps by other potteries in the first quarter of the nineteenth century.[6] As the decoration appears to be an early nineteenth-century one, the question as to the use of this mark becomes pertinent. Was 'WOOD' impressed possibly used at times during Enoch Wood's partnership with James Caldwell (c. 1790–1818)? Or is this the mark of some other Wood? The Wood family was well represented in the Staffordshire potteries. In any case, this cup and saucer stands as an example of a competitor's adaptation of another pottery's successful transfer-printed decoration.

Another well-regarded Staffordshire potter, John Shorthose, also made yellow-glazed wares. Shorthose's working dates were from about 1785 to about 1823, but the periods during which the various Shorthose marks were in use have not been fully determined. There seems to have been some over-lapping in the use of the Shorthose marks, possibly reflecting interests in more than one pottery. The strawberry dish and stand in plate XXXIV has the

6. See Geoffrey A. Godden, *Encyclopedia of British Pottery and Porcelain Marks* (Herbert Jenkins Ltd, London and Crown Publishers, Inc., New York 1964), p.736.

impressed I. SHORTHOSE mark. This eight-sided dish stands on claw feet and has a border neatly pierced with heart shapes, with rim lines in black enamel; it dates from the late eighteenth or early nineteenth century. A number of other marked Shorthose pieces are known, including children's toy tea services, teapots (figure 38), and bowls (figure 39). Surviving marked Shorthose pieces are lustred, decorated in enamel colours, or transfer-printed in red or black. Pastoral scenes and scenes of children playing seem to have been favoured by this pottery. There appear to be no extant records of Shorthose & Co. (c. 1817–32) or its predecessors, and little has been written about this important early nineteenth-century pottery. From the comparatively large number of marked pieces to be found, it seems that Shorthose & Co. made considerable amounts of yellow-glazed wares.

One short-lived pottery operated by Thomas Harley in Lane End (c. 1802–08) evidently made a speciality of relief diamond-quilted pearlware jugs, upon which the alternating diamonds were painted in silver lustre. A number of these pieces, sometimes called 'harlequin jugs', are impressed 'HARLEY' or 'T. HARLEY'. The large jug in plate XXXV of the same design but with an overall yellow glaze with alternate diamonds painted in silver lustre, can be reasonably attributed to Harley. The firm of John and George Rogers of Longport (1784–1814) or the successor firm, John Rogers & Son (1814–36), also produced yellow-glazed earthenware. The plate in figure 40 can be attributed to this firm on the basis of its panelled border with relief floral

39. Bowl printed in black with scenes of children at play. Mark: 'Shorthose & Co.' in cursive black over the glaze. c. 1810. Diameter 6¾ inches.

40. Plate with a panelled border containing relief floral sprays. Border and flowers in the centre painted in brown, red and green. Probably John Rogers & Sons. c. 1815-25. Diameter 7 inches.

sprays. Similar pearlware plates with the impressed mark 'ROGERS' are not uncommon. The miniature part dinner service (figure 41) probably made for children's play, has pieces with one of the marks used by Samuel Alcock & Co. (c. 1828–53). Printed with oriental scenes, this play service probably dates c. 1830–40. The pair of cup plates in plate XXXVI are painted in black, iron-red and green. The names 'George' and 'Henry' perhaps indicate these were made for children. These cup plates are impressed 'Hackwood', a mark that still defies precise attribution since several potters of this name were working in Staffordshire in the early nineteenth century.[7] Though there may be confusion as to the exact maker, these cup plates are evidence of yet another pottery manufacturing yellow-glazed wares.

Thus, on the basis of marked pieces or firm attributions, a total of nine Staffordshire potteries can be demonstrated to have made yellow-glazed earthenware, and it is probable that other Staffordshire potteries also did so.

Leaving Staffordshire, the next largest known pottery manufacturing yellow-glazed wares was the Rockingham Pottery (Brameld) in Swinton, Yorkshire. The considerable output of quality earthenwares by this pottery from the mid-eighteenth century until 1842 included some yellow-glazed earthenware, of which one marked piece is known.[8] This is a jug and cover, moulded overall

7. *Ibid,* p.299.
8. See Dennis G. Rice, *The Illustrated Guide to Rockingham Pottery and Porcelain* (Barrie & Jenkins Ltd, London and Praeger Publishers, New York 1971), p.24 and fig.51.

with a pineapple pattern and enamel-painted over the yellow glaze with red stars on each diamond and with blue rim lines and details on the handles and finial (plate XXXVII). Another jug in the Leon Collection with the same diamond relief design and distinctive herringbone-patterned handle also can be attributed to Rockingham.

The north of England supported a substantial pottery industry in the late eighteenth and early nineteenth centuries. From the standpoint of quality, Hartley, Greens & Company's Leeds Pottery was probably the most important, producing creamwares that equalled or surpassed the creamwares of Wedgwood and other Staffordshire factories. The marked or attributed yellow-glazed pieces from the Leeds Pottery reflect this high standard. Perhaps the earliest of the Leeds yellow-glazed wares are the pair of melon-shaped tureens in plate XXXVIII dating about 1785 and impressed 'LEEDS * POTTERY'. The leaf-shaped stands are attached to the lower parts of the tureens and the

41. Miniature part dinner service printed in brown with oriental scenes and overpainted in colours. Mark: Beehive and 'ALCOCK' impressed. c. 1830-40. Platter 2¼ inches long.

42. Dish with a pierced cover, painted in red and with silver lustre. Mark: 'LEEDS POTTERY' impressed. c. 1800-10. 4 inches high.

43. Medallion of the painter Le Seueur, overpainted in black and red. Mark: 'Leeds Pottery' impressed. c. 1800-10. 2⅝ inches high.

moulded leaves and bud finials are delicately outlined in light green. Tureens of this shape were illustrated in the Leeds Pattern Book of 1783.[9] From the early nineteenth century, and also marked, comes a small Leeds dish with an intricately moulded and pierced cover (figure 42). Another piece with precisely patterned pierced decoration is a yellow-glazed plate with a stencilled leaf design in silver lustre (plate XXXIX). Though unmarked, comparison with creamware examples and with illustrations in the Leeds Pattern Book would seem to justify a Leeds attribution for this plate. The Leeds Pottery also made medallions in the style of Wedgwood, though to a far lesser degree. The small medallion in figure 43, yellow overall and painted in black and red, is a marked Leeds Pottery piece depicting the French painter Le Seueur. The basket and stand in plate XL, though unmarked, can be attributed to Leeds; the moulded details duplicate creamware ones made by Hartley, Greens & Company. The two-handled presentation cup with 'Jonathan Hawksworth' painted in black on one side and '1812' on the reverse, in plate XLI, has strong Leeds characteristics and can be attributed with some degree of certainty to that pottery. Two-handled presentation cups seem to have been something of a speciality at Leeds. This one is of a typical Leeds shape and is decorated in black and red with a grape vine motif that matches a design in one of the Leeds pattern books (figure 44).[10] The association appears to be corroborated by the notation beneath the pattern, 'Yellow Glaze—Line at Foot'. This bit of documentary evidence has another implication: the fact that the Leeds Pattern Book specifically mentions yellow glaze implies with some authority that yellow-glazed wares were not necessarily exceptional production items, but part of the regular line, though no doubt made in small quantities.

9. See Donald Towner, *The Leeds Pottery* (Cory, Adams & Mackay Ltd, London 1963), reprint of 1783 Pattern Book, p.16, no.68. For similar Leeds melon tureens in creamware, but with pierced covers, see Kidson and Kidson, pl.7.
10. *Leeds Pattern Book for Enamelled Teawares,* 1819. Collection of the Leeds Museum.

44. Drawing from the *Leeds Pattern Book for Enamelled Teawares,* 1819. *Courtesy of the Leeds City Libraries*

The two-handled bowl in figure 45, printed in black with trophies, is of later date. It has the impressed marks 'HARTLEY GREENS & CO' and 'LEEDS ★ POTTERY', which were in use until the firm's bankruptcy in 1820. The legend 'INDEPENDENCIA OU MORTE' refers to Brazil's revolution and independence from Portugal in 1822. The flags among the trophies follow the design of Brazil's flag (1822–89). It seems probable that this piece was decorated a few years after it was manufactured and was part of a service or group of pieces decorated in commemoration of Brazil's independence. Several yellow-glazed pieces with the same decoration are in the collection of the Museu Histórico Nacional in Rio de Janeiro.[11]

There were other potteries in the north of England making yellow-glazed earthenware, modest pieces in most cases. Thomas Fell & Company's St Peter's Pottery in Newcastle-upon-Tyne was one such manufacture, making both transfer-printed and enamel-decorated wares. The small plate in figure 46, transfer-printed in black with flowers, is marked 'FELL' and dates from about 1820. Other Fell pieces have the 'F' and anchor mark used about 1817 to 1830. Especially interesting among these is the souvenir plate in figure 47; the German texts around the design read 'Steamship from Hamburg to London' and 'A Present for My Daughter'. This modest little plate is decorated by all three methods, lustre, enamel painting, and transfer-printing.

The Sunderland Pottery, located in Sunderland, Co. Durham and operated by various proprietors from 1807 to 1865, was well known for its transfer-printed pink lustre wares and also made some yellow-glazed wares. One marked piece is the Burdett jug described in Chapter IV (figure 17), but other pieces can be attributed to the Sunderland Pottery on the basis of form

11. This information was supplied by the Hon. Joaquim de Sousa-Leão of Rio de Janeiro.

45. Two-handled bowl printed in black with trophies, probably commemorating Brazilian independence. Marks: 'HARTLEY GREENS & CO' 'LEEDS ★ POTTERY' impressed. c. 1820. 3¾ inches high, diameter 8¾ inches.

and decoration. There is a fine yellow-glazed pitcher in the collection of the Yorkshire Museum, printed with a view of a ship and signed 'PHILLIPS & CO' 'SUNDERLAND POTTERY'. John Phillips appears to have leased the pottery as early as 1807 and to have been an owner (perhaps in partnership) from about 1813 until 1819; the mark 'PHILLIPS & CO.' was apparently used during these six years. Another marked Sunderland jug, which is in the Leon Collection, is transfer-printed in black on one side with a Masonic design and on the other with a ship and the legend 'Success to the COAL TRADE' (figure 48).[12] Transfer-printed jugs with scenes of 'The Tythe Pig' (figure 49) have the same shape as the marked jug in the Yorkshire Museum and the Burdett jug previously discussed. Also, the three concentric lines at the neck, which appear characteristic of Sunderland, are found on all these jugs. An

46. Plate printed in black with a floral design. Mark: 'FELL' impressed. c. 1820. Diameter 6 inches.

12. See J. T. Shaw, ed, *The Potteries of Sunderland and District* (County Borough of Sunderland, 3rd edn, Sunderland 1968), pp.22-3.

47. Plate decorated with copper lustre, transfer-printing and enamel painting. Mark: 'FELL' impressed. c. 1820. Diameter 8 inches.

48. Jug transfer-printed in black with a collier and the legend 'Success to the COAL TRADE'. Mark: 'PHILLIPS & CO' 'SUNDERLAND POTTERY'. c. 1815. 6 inches high.

attribution to the Sunderland Pottery (c. 1815–20) does not seem unreasonable, since these particular shapes, handles and neck decorations are most distinctive.

The yellow-glazed mug in figure 50, of about 1810, can be given a reasonably firm attribution on the basis of its transfer-printed decoration of 'The Battle of the Nile'. This particular print and the accompanying caption and verse comprise a special version used by John Dawson & Co. of Sunderland (c. 1799–1864). Though this important naval victory of the Napoleonic Wars was widely celebrated in contemporary English ceramics, a marked Dawson jug in the Sunderland Museum collection provides a specific link.[13] Not only is the print on the marked piece identical, but the spelling and punctuation in the verse and the errors in the caption also match verbatim.[14] In the same manner, the yellow-glazed teapot in plate XLII, printed with a scene after Adam Buck, can be attributed to Dawson & Co. on the basis of the same print appearing on a marked Dawson pearlware cup and saucer dated about 1815, in the Victoria and Albert Museum.[15]

Two Adam Buck drawings lead to the attribution of a large number of pieces to Robert Maling's Ouseburn Pottery in Newcastle. This pottery, established in 1817, made lustred and printed earthenwares. An engraved copper printing plate (figure 51), now in the collection of the Laing Museum, has descended in the Maling family. The three views on the printing plate,

13. *Ibid.,* fig.3.
14. The caption reads 'Lord Nelson Engaging the Toulon Fleet of [sic] the Mouths [sic] of the Nile'. See James Crawley, ed., *Rhymes and Mottoes on Sunderland Pottery* (County Borough of Sunderland, Sunderland 1960), p.31, no.183.
15. Illustrated in Geoffrey A. Godden, *An Illustrated Encyclopedia of British Pottery and Porcelain* (Barrie & Jenkins Ltd, London and Crown Publishers, Inc., New York 1966), p.126, fig.205. A Dawson & Co. bowl in the Metropolitan Museum of Art printed with the same view is illustrated in John and Baker, ill.77D.

49. Jug printed in black with 'The Tythe Pig'. Probably J. Phillips & Co., Sunderland. c. 1815-20. 5 inches high.

XLI. Two-handled cup painted in black, red and green. Probably Leeds. Dated 1812. 5 inches high.

XLII. Teapot and cover printed in red with a scene after Adam Buck. Probably John Dawson & Co, Sunderland. c. 1815-20. 6 inches high.

XLIII. Jug printed in black
and overpainted in red and
green and silver lustre.
Herculaneum Pottery,
Liverpool. c. 1810.
14½ inches high.

XLIV. Jug painted in black,
red and green. Possibly
Bristol. c. 1825-35.
4 inches high.

XLV. Footed punch bowl
decorated with copper
lustre and painted in
black, green and yellow.
Probably Cambrian Pottery,
Swansea. c. 1824-31.
8 inches high.

XLVI. Jug printed in
black and overpainted in
enamel colours with a bull-
baiting scene. Probably
Glamorgan Pottery.
c. 1815-25. $5\frac{1}{2}$ inches high.

XLVII. Jug printed in
black and overpainted in
enamel colours with a
scene of Sir Toby Philpott.
Probably Glamorgan
Pottery. c. 1815-25.
$7\frac{3}{4}$ inches high.

XLVIII. A group of yellow-
glazed earthenware animals
and bird figures. Late 18th
and early 19th century.
Squirrel 5 inches high.

XLIX. Two sheep with details picked out in black and green. Early 19th century. Figure on the right $6\frac{3}{8}$ inches long.

L. Pair of lions. Early 19th century. 9 inches high, 12 inches long.

LI. Bust of Shakespeare
painted in brown, iron-red,
orange and green. Possibly
Enoch Wood. c. 1810–20.
$8\frac{1}{2}$ inches high.

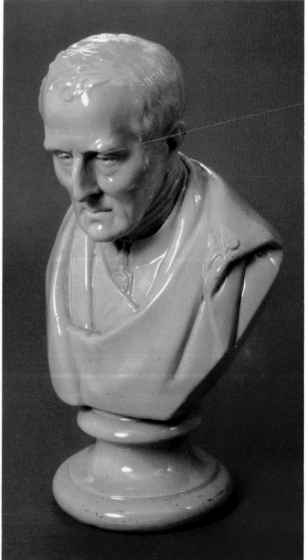

LII. Bust of Wellington as
an old man. Signed 'Joseph
Pitts'. Parian ware covered
with an overall yellow glaze.
Dated 1852. 9 inches high.

LIII. Quill or toothpick
holders in the shape of a
porcupine and rooster.
Early 19th century.
Rooster 4 inches high.

LIV. Box in the shape of
woman's head. Possibly Leeds
Pottery. Late 18th century.
Height 3¾ inches.

LV. Antony and Cleopatra.
Probably Dillwyn & Co.,
Swansea. c. 1820. Antony
12½ inches long.

LVI. A group of yellow-
glazed children's mugs.
c. 1800–40. Bird mug
2 inches high.

Text on mug: of France ...s in vain / Lord Nelson Running the French Fleet of the Mouth of the Nile / When Nelson appears his ... That Britons are ...

50. Mug printed in black with 'The Battle of the Nile'. John Dawson & Co., Sunderland. c. 1810. 5 inches high.

after Buck, depict typical empire-dressed ladies and children at the piano, on a see saw, and on a Grecian couch. The print of the lady at the piano was used extensively on tea services (figure 20). The second view on the engraved plate, of the lady on the Grecian couch with two children playing at her feet, appears in the vase in figure 52, and this makes a Maling association probable.

The St Anthony's Pottery in Newcastle, while under the proprietorship of Sewell & Donkin (1828–52), also made yellow-glazed earthenware. Again, the popularity of prints after Adam Buck may be seen in the marked plate in figure 53. Certainly, from the marked and reasonably attributed pieces, it can be said that the north-eastern counties produced a respectable portion of the English yellow-glazed earthenware, comparable in both quality and quantity with that from Staffordshire.

Liverpool and its environs comprised a most important ceramics manufacturing centre in the eighteenth and early nineteenth centuries. Delft tablewares and tiles, porcelain, and a variety of earthenwares and stonewares were made there. Though no marked Liverpool yellow-glazed earthenware is presently known, a number of pieces can be attributed to the Herculaneum Pottery (c. 1796–1833). Perhaps the most important of these is a group of three very

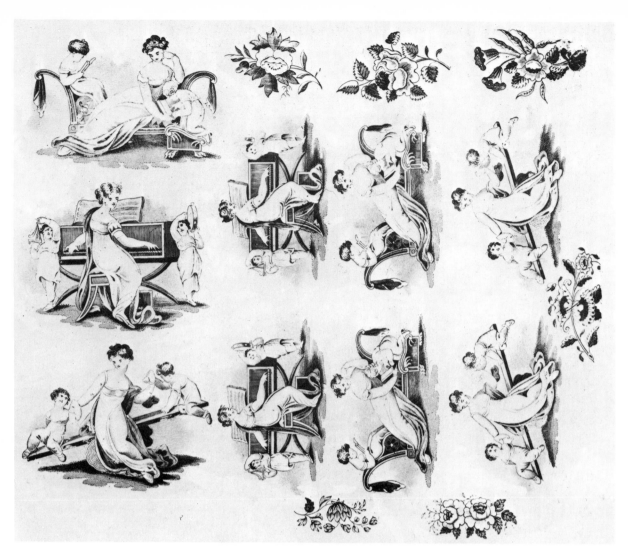

51. Pull from a copper printing plate probably engraved by Adam Buck. *Courtesy of the Laing Museum, Newcastle*

large, yellow-glazed jugs, transfer-printed and overpainted in enamel colours.[16] One of these jugs is in the Leon Collection (plate XLIII); it is printed with eleven views which have been overpainted in red and green. These prints include farm scenes, hunting scenes, the seasons 'Spring' and 'Summer' and under the spout 'The Farmer's Arms' and an appropriate verse. These transfer prints were used by the Herculaneum factory. Though similar prints were used by other potteries, there were variations in the engraved scenes. In specific detail the transfer prints on this jug match known Herculaneum ones, the key print being the one of 'The Farmer's Arms' and the accompanying verse ending 'Long life and success to the farmer'.[17]

Several transfer-printed pieces with American views may also be given Liverpool attributions, and these are discussed in Chapter VIII. Another example that may be assigned to the Herculaneum Pottery is the mug in figure 54, printed in black with a scene entitled 'The Politicians'. The same

16. In the collection of the City of Liverpool Museums, the Eugene Sussel Collection, and the Leon Collection.
17. See Alan Smith, *The Illustrated Guide to Liverpool Herculaneum Pottery* (Barrie & Jenkins, London 1970), p.38, figs.66 and 67.

52. Vase printed in black
with a scene after Adam
Buck. Probably Robert
Maling, Newcastle.
c. 1815-20. 4 inches high.

53. Plate printed in black
with a scene after Adam
Buck. 'SEWELL &
DONKIN' impressed (St
Anthony's Pottery,
Newcastle). c. 1830-5.
Diameter $8\frac{1}{4}$ inches.

print is on an attributed Herculaneum creamware jug in the collections of the Liverpool City Museums. The names of the two newspapers at the feet of the politicians, *The Argus* and *The Oracle*, suggest a date of about 1800.[18] The jug in figure 55 printed on one side with a version of 'Come Box the Compass' and on the reverse with a ship and the frequently used legend 'Success to the Wooden Walls of Old England', also has possible Liverpool connections. The transfer-print is signed 'I. Johnson, Liverpool'. A number of other signed Johnson transfer-prints are known, but the exact identity and activities of J. Johnson of Liverpool remains uncertain.[19] There were at least three Joseph Johnsons active in Liverpool at roughly the same time. For the present, it is not unreasonable to attribute this mug and other signed Johnson pieces to Liverpool, possibly the Herculaneum Pottery.[20] As large amounts of Staffordshire cream-coloured wares were printed in Liverpool, the possibility that some Staffordshire yellow-glazed wares also were printed there cannot be discounted.

18. *The Argus* was published from 1789 to 1791 and again in 1828. *The Oracle* was published from 1788 to 1802.
19. For a list of the Johnson signed pieces and a discussion of Joseph Johnson, see Smith, pp.34-8.
20. A drinking cup (beaker) with the same 'Come Box the Compass' print also signed 'I. Johnson Liverpool' is in the Schreiber Collection at the Victoria and Albert Museum. Schreiber Catalogue, p.83, no.413.

54. Mug printed in black with a scene entitled 'The Politicians'. Possibly Herculaneum Pottery, Liverpool. c. 1800. 4 inches high.

55. Jug printed in black with 'Come Box the Compass'. The print is signed 'I. Johnson Liverpool'. Possibly Liverpool. c. 1800-20. 4¾ inches high.

56. Pair of jugs printed in red with Napoleonic War cartoons, the prints signed 'Jas. Brindley Des. & Eng.' Cambrian Pottery, Swansea. c. 1812. Larger jug 6½ inches high.

One piece, a barrel-shaped jug (plate XLIV) dating about 1825–35, may well have a Bristol association, the barrel shape being favoured at Bristol.

There is every indication that the Welsh production of yellow-glazed earthenwares was considerable. Though marked pieces are rare, many examples can be attributed to two Swansea manufacturers, the Cambrian Pottery and the Glamorgan Pottery. The Cambrian Pottery, which dates back to the mid-eighteenth century, came under the management of L. W. Dillwyn in 1802 and remained under his and his son's proprietorship (except for a lease to Timothy and John Bevington from 1817 to 1824) until 1850. A wide variety of pottery and porcelain was made there, and to judge from the quantity of surviving pieces, the Cambrian Pottery was a major producer of yellow-glazed earthenwares. The pair of yellow-glazed jugs in figure 56, transfer-printed in red with Napoleonic War cartoons, was most probably made at the Cambrian Pottery.[21] They have Swansea characteristics in the construction of the base, the high shoulders, and the rather small handle attached high on the piece. The transfer-prints, with the legends 'Bonaparte Dethron'd' and 'Peace and Plenty' around the necks, are signed 'Jas. Brindley Des. & Eng.'. Brindley, an independent engraver, evidently worked at Swansea at certain times, providing transfer-printing plates for the decoration of both earthenwares and porcelain. Another copper plate engraver who was active at Swansea was Thomas Rothwell. This experienced decorator had worked in Staffordshire before coming to Wales in about 1790. The decoration on the

21. Nance, pp.106, 539-40 and pl.LII A,B.

57. Jug transfer-printed in black with a Prince of Wales feathers design, from an engraving by Thomas Rothwell. Cambrian Pottery, Swansea. c. 1810. $5\frac{3}{4}$ inches high.

58. Jug printed in red with birds and feathers after Thomas Bewick. Probably Cambrian Pottery, Swansea. c. 1820-30. $4\frac{1}{4}$ inches high.

jug in figure 57 printed in black on one side with the Prince of Wales feathers and on the reverse with a view of a castle, was perhaps executed by Rothwell.[22] The linked chain border on the neck of this jug is found in other Cambrian Pottery pieces. A large footed punch bowl (plate XLV) can also be attributed to this factory; dating from about 1824-31, this piece has the same shape and moulded relief pattern found on marked transfer-printed wares from the Cambrian Pottery.[23] The distinctive hand-painted foliate design and accompanying copper lustre border on this punch bowl is duplicated in a number of other forms including smaller footed punch bowls, plates, wash bowls, and butter tubs (figure 29). On the basis of this decoration, there are grounds for attributing all pieces painted in this manner to Swansea. The small jug in figure 58, finely printed in red with birds after Thomas Bewick, can also be assigned a Cambrian Pottery provenance. Its shape is typical of Swansea jugs, and the

22. For a similar creamware jug, see Nance, pl.LI F, 1. A sketchy biography of Rothwell appears in Nance, pp. 477-9. For a more recent study on this artist-engraver, see E. Norman Stretton, 'Thomas Rothwell, Engraver and Copper Plate Printer, 1740-1807', *Transactions of the English Ceramics Circle* (London 1967), Vol.6, Part 3, pp.249-53. Plate 154 in this article illustrates a Swansea earthenware coffee pot printed with the feathers design.
23. See Nance, pl.LXV A,B.

meticulously printed feather border on the neck was a Swansea decorative convention used both on earthenware and porcelain.[24] A mark consisting of an impressed 'D' (possibly for Dillwyn) has sometimes been attributed to the Cambrian Pottery; it is found on the octagonal cup plate decorated with a bird in silver lustre in figure 59.

The Glamorgan Pottery, also located in Swansea, manufactured earthenwares from about 1813 to 1839. Certain yellow-glazed jugs may be attributed to Glamorgan on the basis of their shapes and decoration. The one in plate XLVI has a bull-baiting scene, again after Thomas Bewick.[25] A Wellington print, and a Toby Philpott drinking scene (plate XLVII), also appear in precisely the same version on marked Glamorgan creamware jugs. The Toby Philpott view was probably copied from an engraving of about 1786 and the verse under the spout is from a song 'The Brown Jug'.[26] On all these jugs the similar handles

24. See Nance, p.102, pl.XLVII; see also Kathleen M. Armistead and W. J. Grant-Davidson, *Catalogue of the Kildare S. Meager Bequest of Swansea Pottery* (Glynn Vivian Art Gallery, Swansea n.d.), no.74, pl.9; W. J. Grant-Davidson, *Swansea Pottery Bi-Centenary Exhibition 1768-1968* (Glynn Vivian Art Gallery, Swansea 1968), no.202, pl.8.
25. From Thomas and John Bewick, *Select Fables; with Cuts Designed and Engraved by Thomas and John Bewick, and Others, Previous to the Year 1784* (London 1820).
26. A mezzotint of Sir Toby printed for and sold by Bowles & Laver of London (n.d.) in the print collection of the British Museum is nearly identical to the Glamorgan print. The song 'The Brown Jug' was written by the Reverend Francis Fawkes and published in 1761. This is probably the first reference to Toby Philpott. See Desmond Eyles, *Good Sir Toby* (Doulton & Co. Ltd, London 1955).

59. Cup plate decorated with silver lustre. Mark: 'D' impressed. Probably Dillwyn & Co., Swansea. c. 1820. Diameter 4 inches.

60. Plate with an
overall daisy pattern in
relief, overpainted with red
and green. Probably
Llanelly Pottery. c. 1840-50.
Diameter 6 inches.

and neck decorations of a vine in black and red are characteristic of the
Glamorgan Pottery.

A third, and later, Welsh pottery evidently made yellow-glazed earthenware. This was the South Wales Pottery which was established in Llanelly in
1839. The small plate in figure 60 decorated in relief with a daisy pattern and
painted in enamel colours, has the same moulded details as marked Llanelly
creamware plates.[27]

This summary of factories manufacturing yellow-glazed wares has only
dealt with marked or reasonably attributable pieces. As the great majority of
yellow-glazed earthenware was unmarked, it appears quite certain that a
number of factories not mentioned here also produced yellow-glazed wares.
Hopefully, as time passes, other marked or attributable pieces will come to
light.

27. See Nance, pl.LXXVII F; Dilys Jenkins, *Llanelly Pottery* (Deb Books, Swansea 1968) facing
     p.33.

CHAPTER SEVEN

Figures, toys, children's mugs

Earthenware figures comprised a part of the production of many leading English potters in the eighteenth and nineteenth centuries. There was a demand for modest figures that were no more than decorative trifles and also for more ambitious figures and figure groups which were made in limited quantities. Yellow-glazed earthenware figures, for the most part, were simple ones but a few impressive models were achieved.

Small figures of animals and birds, both domestic and wild, enjoyed great popularity, and a variety of these were made in yellow glaze. Though none can be attributed with certainty to the eighteenth century, several are closely related to eighteenth-century models. The rooster with his head tucked under his wing, in plate XLVIII, is taken from a model of the Whieldon type,[1] and the songbird is similar in composition to Whieldon-type birds and to English porcelain ones made at Chelsea and Bow.[2] The imperious eagle (also plate XLVIII) is quite unusual. Reclining sheep were also made by many potteries and seem to be the most ubiquitous of all the English ceramic animals. Yellow glaze versions are not uncommon, but most were poorly modelled and decorated only with yellow glaze, though occasionally details in overglaze enamel colours were added (plate XLIX). Other animals found in yellow-glazed earthenware are dogs, squirrels, and lions—the small lion with oriental features (in plate XLVIII) is rare. Strangely, it appears that no yellow-glazed cats were made, though the cat was one of the commonest animal figures produced at the time. Perhaps the most impressive animal figures made in yellow glaze are the large pair of lions in plate L standing on rectangular bases. Originally derived from the

1. See Cyril Earle, *The Earle Collection of Early Staffordshire Pottery* (A. Brown & Sons, Ltd, London 1915), p.103, no.188.
2. Compare with a Whieldon-type songbird illustrated in Herbert Read, *Staffordshire Pottery Figures* (Duckworth & Co. Ltd, London and Houghton Mifflin Company, Boston and New York 1929), pl.27.

well-known pair of sculptured bronze lions in the Loggia dei Lanzi in Florence, this yellow-glazed earthenware version, dating from the first quarter of the nineteenth century, has more direct ancestors in similar English earthenware lions, perhaps made as early as 1760–70.[3]

The range of human figures was also limited. As might be expected, the 'Four Seasons' were made in several sizes. The figures of Spring and Autumn in figure 61 are identical in size and moulded details to sets of the seasons decorated in colours and purple lustre made at the Sunderland Pottery, and impressed Dixon, Austin & Co.,[4] so it seems justifiable to attribute these yellow-glazed figures to that firm. Two historical figures deserve mention. The poorly modelled Admiral Rodney in figure 62 possibly dates from the eighteenth century, since Rodney's major victories (at Cape St Vincent and Saintes)

3. For a lion of this type attributed to Ralph Wood, see Ross E. Taggart, *Catalogue of the Burnap Collection* (Nelson Gallery-Atkins Museum, rev. edn, Kansas City, Missouri 1967), no.390. See also Harold Mackintosh, *Early English Figure Pottery* (Chapman & Hall Ltd, London 1938), p.29, no.101.
4. Compare John and Baker, colour illus.81.

61. 'Spring' and 'Autumn'. Probably Dixon, Austin & Co., Sunderland. c. 1830. 'Spring' 8 inches high.

62. Admiral Rodney,
possibly after a model by
Ralph Wood, Jr. Late 18th
or early 19th century.
$6\frac{1}{4}$ inches high.

63. A mounted Hessian.
Early 19th century.
4¼ inches high.

occurred in the early 1780s and he himself died in 1792. This figure was probably copied from a model of Rodney that has been attributed to the pottery of the Ralph Woods.[5] As the elder Wood died in 1772 the prototype of this figure would have been the work of Ralph Wood, Jr. Another figure that may be the work of the Wood family is the bust of Shakespeare in plate LI. Well modelled and painted, it is similar to a creamware bust of Shakespeare attributed to Enoch Wood in the collections of the Art Institute of Chicago. The modelling of the pedestal and the quality of the overglaze painting lend support to such an attribution.[6] The bust of Wellington as an elderly man, modelled by Joseph Pitts (plate LII) is of interest as a peculiarity. Dating 1852, and thus later than the yellow-glazed wares discussed here, this piece is made of parian ware, not earthenware.[7] The overall yellow glaze appears similar both in composition and effect, and the piece itself provides an example of the contribution of overall yellow glaze on a newer ceramic body. Also military in character is the toy-like figure of a mounted Hessian soldier in figure 63. This particular model was sometimes given an overall green glaze.[8] The yellow-glazed group of a mother and child, perhaps Virgin and Child, in figure 64 is quite rare; it bears some resemblance to a composition of the Virgin and Child attributed to Wood and Caldwell.[9] The bust of a young girl in figure 65, with painted details, represents a less formal type of yellow-glazed figure.

Some yellow-glazed figures served utilitarian purposes. Whistles in the shape of birds (figure 66), banks in the shape of dogs, and quill (or toothpick?) holders (plate LIII) in the shape of roosters or porcupines fall within this group. Another useful object is a box, with a screw cap at the base, in the shape of a woman's head (plate LIV). Perhaps intended as a patch box or a snuff box, this piece probably dates from the end of the eighteenth century and possibly was manufactured at the Leeds Pottery. An identical box in pearlware has been given a Leeds Pottery attribution and dated about 1790.[10] The probable prototype for these boxes can be found in a similar one of English porcelain, probably Lowestoft, which is in the collections of the Victoria and Albert Museum.

Though most of the yellow-glazed figures were modest in both size and composition, there were exceptions. In addition to the pair of lions previously described, two large, reclining figures of Antony and Cleopatra in plate LV also are impressive. Antony's antecedents are obscure, but Cleopatra has an involved derivation. The prototype is apparently a Greek figure of Ariadne from which Roman copies were made. By the beginning of the eighteenth century a transition had occurred and engravings of bronzes of that period

5. Robert K. Price, *Astbury, Whieldon and Ralph Wood Figures and Toby Jugs* (The Bodley Head Ltd, London 1922), p.68, no.30, pl.XXXIII, no.30.
6. However, for a slightly different version, also attributed to Enoch Wood, see Taggart, p.143, no.552.
7. For another version in parian of Wellington as an old man, see Geoffrey Bemrose, *Nineteenth Century English Pottery and Porcelain* (Faber and Faber Ltd, London 1952), fig.75. A parian group by Joseph Pitts is illustrated in the same book, fig.76.
8. An identical figure, but with an overall green glaze, is in the collections of Colonial Williamsburg.
9. See Read, pl.52.
10. See Towner, *The Leeds Pottery*, fig.31A. Some creamware boxes of this type were reproduced in the 1960s.

64. Group of a mother and
child. Early 19th century.
3⅝ inches high.

LVII. Medallion printed in black with a portrait of George Washington. Probably Herculaneum Pottery, Liverpool. c. 1800. 5 inches high.

LVIII. Beaker printed in black with a portrait of Benjamin Franklin. c. 1800, 3½ inches high.

LIX. Jug printed in black
with 'America'. c. 1800–20.
8½ inches high.

LX. Mug printed in black
with a map of eastern
North America. c. 1800–10.
6 inches high.

LXI. Jug printed in brown
with the arms of the
United States. c. 1810–20.
7 inches high.

LXII. Jug printed in black
with various American
symbols. Dated 1815.
$4\frac{3}{4}$ inches high.

LXIII. Jug printed in black with the Great Seal of the United States and a ribbon containing the names of ten states and 'Boston'. c. 1810-20. 7½ inches high.

LXIV. Plate painted with the Great Seal of the United States in black, red and green. c. 1810-25. Diameter 6¼ inches.

65. Bust of a young girl.
Early 19th century.
4 inches high.

show the same figure captioned as Cleopatra. With an asp entwined around her left arm, the reclining figure clearly became Cleopatra in late eighteenth-century England. Numerous potters, including Ralph Wood, Jr and Enoch Wood, made these figures.[11] Though unmarked, the attribution of the yellow-glazed pair to Dillwyn & Co. of Swansea seems justified since there is an identical pair of yellow-glazed figures in the National Museum of Wales, with 'SWANSEA' impressed in the base of the Cleopatra.[12] The similar Cleopatra figure in figure 67, covered overall with a silver lustre wash, can also be given a Swansea attribution.

Small earthenware mugs specifically made as gifts for children enjoyed wide popularity in England during the first half of the nineteenth century. Most of these were creamware or pearlware decorated with transfer-prints, and less frequently hand-painted with overglaze enamel colours or lustre. To a lesser extent, small beakers were made. Yellow-glazed earthenware children's mugs were evidently produced in quantity and many have survived. They were most probably made by a number of potteries, but attributions are rarely possible. The decoration of these mugs and beakers was stereotyped (plate LVI and figure 68). Monogram initials and Christian names comprise one group. Often

11. For example, see the Earle Collection Catalogue, p.191, figs.132, 535, 537 and 541.
12. See Nance, pl.XXXIII.

66. Two whistles in the shape of birds. Early 19th century. Decorated bird 3 inches high.

67. Cleopatra, the yellow glaze covered by a silver lustre wash. Probably Dillwyn & Co, Swansea. c. 1820. 11 inches long.

68. Two children's beakers. c. 1800-40. 2¾ inches high.

69. Three children's mugs with transfer-printed decoration. c. 1800–40. 'Mimicry' 2½ inches high.

70. Miniature pieces probably used as toys or for dolls' houses. Decorated in enamel colours and silver lustre. c. 1800–25. Mug on right 1¼ inches high. The covered dish, compote and tea bowl and saucer are marked 'I. SHORTHOSE'.

the legend 'A present for Jack' or 'A gift for Ann' was incorporated in the design. The 'A.B.C.s' and various mottoes were also popular. Other designs pictured toys and animals. The sources of some of these prints can be traced: for example, the print of a rocking horse in figure 69 was evidently taken from a set of cards showing various toys and probably used to teach spelling or just for play.[13] Other mugs took a moralistic tone. Scenes of unfortunate children being thrown by a horse, kicked by a donkey (figure 69), and tossed by a bull were taken from a children's book discouraging the teasing of animals.[14] Some of the transfer-prints on children's mugs, as might be expected, were copied from the Thomas Bewick woodcuts of animals and birds (figure 69).[15]

13. See Wallis, *Emblematic Cards for the Amusement of Youth* (1788).
14. Elizabeth Turner, *The Cowslip or More Cautionary Stories in Verse* (1811). The wood engravings illustrating this book were by Samuel Williams.
15. The monkey holding a mirror (figure 69) is from Thomas Bewick, *A General History of Quadrupeds* (Longman, Hurst, Rees, Orme & Brown, London 1811), pl.32, fig.8.

Even smaller mugs, part tea services, and other serving pieces (figure 70) were probably toys intended for little girls' play at giving tea parties. Some of the very small miniatures were possibly intended as furnishings for dolls' houses. A few of these miniatures, decorated in enamel colours and silver lustre, are impressed 'I. SHORTHOSE'. In addition to the toy tea things, there were other yellow-glazed objects that probably were intended as toys or as gifts for children. These include whistles, money boxes, baskets, and miniature chairs and cradles (figure 71).

71. A group of toys. c. 1800-40. Chair $3\frac{1}{2}$ inches high.

CHAPTER EIGHT

American views

'American Views' is a term of convenience. After the American Revolution, the English ceramic industry continued to export large quantities of useful wares to the United States. This trade, of course, has endured to the present times. Some of these exported ceramics were decorated with subjects designed to appeal to American buyers. Cityscapes and landscapes, architectural views, portraits of American political leaders and heroes, military and naval scenes, and patriotic emblems comprise the usual subject matter of these American views. For the most part, this type of decoration was transfer-printed. During the period 1785–1850, most American views on earthenware were printed under the glaze in blue (and later in other colours). Such important firms as Enoch Wood & Sons, James and Ralph Clews, and John and William Ridgway conducted a substantial trade in these wares. Creamwares and pearlwares with American views printed or painted over the glaze were exported in lesser quantities. Rather inaccurately, some collectors and dealers categorize these two general types as 'Staffordshire' and 'Liverpool'.[1] Yellow-glazed earthenwares decorated with American views are notable for their rarity. In nearly every case, similar printed or painted decoration can be found in far greater numbers on clear-glazed, cream-coloured earthenwares and pearlwares. The very few American subjects on yellow-glazed wares are not aberrations: rather they reflect the comparatively meagre production of all yellow-glazed wares by the English potteries.

The oval medallion in plate LVII printed in black with a portrait of George

1. The standard reference works on American views are Ellouise Baker Larsen, *American Historical Views on Staffordshire China* (Doubleday & Company, Inc., rev. edn, Garden City, N.Y. 1950) which deals primarily with underglaze printed wares, and Robert H. McCauley, *Liverpool Transfer Designs on Anglo-American Pottery* (The Southworth-Anthoensen Press, Portland, Maine 1942) which is concerned with overglaze printed wares.

Washington and perhaps the only extant example in yellow, can be attributed to the Herculaneum Pottery in Liverpool. The portrait is after Gilbert Stuart, and the engraver of the copper printing plate no doubt copied a contemporary print. This medallion probably dates about 1800, and it may have been made as a memorial shortly after Washington's death in 1799. The Herculaneum attribution rests upon a number of creamware jugs decorated beneath the spout with the identical oval print. Some of these jugs have the impressed mark 'HERCULANEUM'.[2]

The beaker in plate LVIII, a shape seldom encountered in English yellow-glazed earthenwares, is printed in black with two American subjects: on the obverse, a fur-hatted Benjamin Franklin labelled 'Benjn Franklin Born at Boston in New England, 17 Jan. 1706. L.L.D.F.R.S.', and on the reverse, a standard print of the Great Seal of the United States.[3] The source of this portrait of Franklin was probably an engraving published in 1784 by Whitworth and Yates of Birmingham. In turn, this engraving seems to have been derived from a 1777 engraving by Augustin de Saint-Auban which was made from a drawing (now lost) by Charles Nicolas Cochin the Younger. The print of the Great Seal of the United States can be found in numerous versions on the printed clear-glazed creamwares and pearlwares of the period, but it is quite rare on yellow-glazed wares.

A symbolic representation of America is printed on both sides of the jug in plate LIX, which also is decorated with silver lustre borders. One could quibble

2. See Alan Smith, fig.90. For a discussion of the Washington medallions, see pp.39, 40 and fig.38. See also McCauley, p.83, no.47, and pl.II.
3. For this same Franklin print on cream-coloured earthenware, see Larsen, no.503 and McCauley, pl.I, no.15.

72. Mug printed in black under the glaze with the American eagle and trophies. Possibly Ralph Hall & Son. c. 1830-5. 2½ inches high.

73. Mug printed in black with a view of the White House (?). c. 1815-25. $3\frac{1}{2}$ inches high.

and say that this theme should be excluded from the category of American views as it does not relate to the history of the colonies or the early republic, but it can be agreed that this print of America represents an iconographical starting point for other American subjects. Allegorical representations of the four continents probably originated during the Renaissance and seem to have been especially favoured by North German and Netherlandish artists. In the seventeenth century this theme was used in ceramic decoration, and by the eighteenth century the continents were produced as figure groups by some European porcelain factories. The continuation of this theme in ceramic decoration into the early nineteenth century is of interest in itself.

The small mug in figure 72 is printed in black under the yellow glaze. Since practically all transfer-prints on yellow-glazed wares were overglaze, this technical difference is noteworthy. The decoration of an eagle, American shield and trophies on a wave-borne shell, and the legend 'To Washington/ The Patriots of/America' is similar to a known design, but there are differences in detail. A cup and saucer in the Ellouise Baker Larsen Collection, the National Museum of History and Technology, Smithsonian Institution, is printed with this design in red and bears the printed mark 'R. Hall & Son' and the pattern name 'Eagle'.[4] Ralph Hall operated a pottery at Swan Bank, Tunstall from about 1822–49. The Hall cup and saucer probably date from the period 1830–49. The close similarity of the prints might indicate that the yellow-glazed mug was also made by Hall & Son, but no firm attribution can be justified on the basis of this comparative evidence.

4. Larsen, no.501.

A view of what is possibly the White House is printed in black on another mug (figure 73). Though badly printed on one of the commonest forms found in yellow-glazed earthenware, this piece is significant because the transfer-print seems to be an unrecorded one. Comparison with prints of the White House prior to the burning in 1814 and immediately after reconstruction suggests that the building depicted is indeed James Hoban's presidential mansion. The presence of a low extension to the left of the building (the Jefferson portico) provides some additional confirmation for this attribution. The rolling hills in the background may be a fanciful addition by the engraver of the copper plate; such artistic modifications of the landscape were a common practice. However, English country houses were popular subjects for transfer-prints on ceramics, and the possibility that this is such a view cannot be dismissed.

One of the better known American subjects depicts a map of the eastern part of North America surrounded by a cluster of patriotic symbols; an iconographical hodge–podge somewhat relieved by numbered references to a legend at the bottom identifying 'Fame', 'Washington securing Liberty to America', and 'Wisdom & Justice dictating to Dr. Franklin'. This print is not uncommon, and can be found in several versions on clear-glazed creamware bowls, pitchers and mugs. Some of these prints, including one on a yellow-glazed pitcher in the collections of the Chicago Art Institute, are signed F. Morris, Shelton. A yellow-glazed mug with this decoration (plate LX) appears somewhat truncated; the copper plate engraving was slightly too large, so that when the decorator applied the inked transfer papers, the encircling wreath ran out of space at both top and bottom.

American patriotic fervour preceding and during the War of 1812 supplied the English manufacturers with new subject matter for decorating pieces intended for sale in the United States. The fact that a war was involved failed to diminish the enterprise of the English potters, who supplied both sides with ceramics printed with appropriate sentiments. The yellow-glazed jug plate LXI, printed in brown with a version of 'The Arms of the United States', typifies this sort of decoration. Complemented by brown enamel borders and details on handle and spout, the meticulous brown overglaze transfer-print contrasts well with the yellow ground. The same print appears on both sides of the pitcher and a wreath surrounding the legend 'Free Trade and Sailors/Their Rights' is beneath the spout. A rare jug of this same period (plate LXII) has a print of a cartouche containing the legend 'Success to the United States of America, 1815'. This is flanked by an Indian on one side and two eagles on the other, above which flies an American flag.[5] Dating about the same time is a third jug (plate LXIII) with elaborate iconography. It is printed in black on both sides with a somewhat belligerent version of the Great Seal of the United States surmounting a coiled ribbon bearing the names of ten states and 'Boston'. The ribbon circlet is flanked by allegorical figures of 'Peace and Plenty', and 'Independence'. The legend 'Peace and Prosperity to America' is printed in a wreath beneath the spout. The rim, spout and handle details, and the borders

5. For a slightly different version of this print see Larsen, no.786.

of the main transfer prints are all painted in strong, silver lustre. Though encountered quite frequently on clear-glazed creamwares and pearlwares, this subject is seldom found on a yellow ground.[6]

Though the majority of American subjects on yellow-glazed wares were transfer-printed, a few enamel-painted and lustered renditions of the Great Seal of the United States were also made. The arts of the early republic—both domestic and imported—reveal the popularity of this decorative device, a popularity attested in ceramics by its ubiquity in Chinese export porcelain and English transfer-printed earthenwares. English clear-glazed pearlwares, especially those edged in blue or green, were sometimes hand-painted with versions of the Great Seal. The cup plate in figure 74 with a feather edge and

6. Similar jugs are in the Rose Collection, Brandeis University, and the Shollenberger Collection, Valley Forge Historical Society. The pitcher illustrated here (figure 136) has been previously illustrated in John and Baker, illus.44E.

74. Cup plate painted with a crude version of the Great Seal of the United States. Mark: eagle and 'ENOCH WOOD & SONS BURSLEM' impressed. c. 1820-30. Diameter 3½ inches.

scale-moulded border has, in its centre, a crude and sketchy Great Seal painted in silver lustre. This small piece has the circular mark of an eagle and 'ENOCH WOOD & SONS BURSLEM' impressed on the back. Enoch Wood & Sons manufactured large quantities of underglaze blue, transfer-printed wares for sale in the American market, many of which are impressed with a similar mark which seems to have been used on wares intended for the United States from about 1818–46. Though the relief border on this cup plate is not without merit, the amateurish painting (which is not necessarily suspect) indicates a considerable range in the quality of decoration in this particular factory's output for the overseas trade. A second plate (plate LXIV) dating about 1810–25 is more competently painted. The deep border has a scaled relief pattern upon which is superimposed an enamelled seven-point star design in black, red and green. The eagle with its accoutrements is painted in shades of black and grey. In concept and feeling this design is similar to the more commonly found ones in pearlware plates of the period, but it is not nearly as well painted as the typical Great Seal found in contemporary Chinese export porcelains.

A few other American subjects on yellow-glazed earthenwares are known. Perhaps the most frequently encountered are small mugs and jugs printed in black or red-brown with vignettes of Washington and Lafayette. These date from about 1824, the year of Lafayette's triumphant return visit to the United States. Small yellow-glazed mugs are occasionally found painted with the names of Adams, Madison or Monroe. Counterparts of these small mugs in creamware and pearlware also exist.

Bibliography

Aiker, Blanche ed. 1800 *Woodcuts by Thomas Bewick and His School* Dover, New York 1962.

Bemrose, Geoffrey *Nineteenth Century English Pottery and Porcelain* Faber and Faber, London 1952.

Bewick, Thomas *A General History of Quadrupeds* Longman, Hurst, Rees, Orme & Brown, London 1811.

Bewick, Thomas and John *Selected Fables; with Cuts, Designed and Engraved by Thomas and John Bewick, and Others, Previous to the Year 1784* London 1820.

Bosanko, W. *Collecting Old Lustre Ware* William Heinemann, London 1916.

Cook, Cyril *The Life and Work of Robert Hancock* Chapman and Hall, London 1948.

Cooper, Ronald G. *English Slipware Dishes, 1650-1850* Alec Tiranti, London 1968.

Crawley, James ed. *Rhymes and Mottoes on Sunderland Pottery* County Borough of Sunderland, Sunderland 1960.

Earle, Cyril *The Earle Collection of Early Staffordshire Pottery* A. Brown & Sons, London 1915.

Evens, William *Art and History of the Potting Business* Shelton 1846 (Victoria and Albert Museum Library).

Eyles, Desmond *Good Sir Toby* Doulton & Co., London 1955.

Finer, Ann and Savage, George *The Selected Letters of Josiah Wedgwood* Cory, Adams & Mackay, London and Born & Hawes, New York 1965.

Fisher, Stanley W. *The Decoration of English Porcelain* Derek Verschoyle, London 1954.

Gilhespy, F. Brayshaw *Derby Porcelain* MacGibbon and Kee, London 1961.

Godden, Geoffrey A. *An Illustrated Encyclopedia of British Pottery and Porcelain* Herbert Jenkins, London and Crown, New York 1966.

Godden, Geoffrey A. *Encyclopedia of British Pottery and Porcelain Marks* Herbert Jenkins, London and Crown, New York 1964.

Gottesman, Rita S. compiler *The Arts and Crafts in New York, 1726-1776* New York Historical Society, New York 1938.

Grant-Davidson, W. J. *Swansea Pottery Bi-Centenary Exhibition, 1768-1968* Glynn Vivian Art Gallery, Swansea 1968.

Grant-Davidson, W. J. and Armistead, Kathleen M. *Catalogue of the Kildare S. Meager Bequest of Swansea Pottery* Glynn Vivian Art Gallery, Swansea, n.d.

Hillier, Bevis (ed. Hugh Honour) *The Social History of the Decorative Arts— Pottery and Porcelain, 1700-1914* Weidenfeld & Nicolson, London and Meredith Press, New York 1968.

Honey, William B. *European Ceramic Art* Faber and Faber, London 1952.

Jenkins, Dilys *Llanelly Pottery* Deb Books, Swansea 1968.

John, William D. and Baker, Warren *Old English Lustre Pottery* R. H. Johns, Newport, Mon. 1951.

Kidson, Joseph R. and Frank *Historical Notices of the Leeds Old Pottery* J. R. Kidson, Leeds 1892.

Lakin, Thomas *The Valuable Receipts of the Late Mr Thomas Lakin, Leeds* Printed for Mrs Lakin by Edward Baines, 1824 (Victoria and Albert Museum Library).

Larsen, Ellouise Baker *American Historical Views on Staffordshire China,* rev. edn. Doubleday, New York 1950.

Leeds Pattern Book for Enamelled Teawares 1819 (Leeds City Public Libraries).

Mackenna, F. Severne *Chelsea Porcelain, The Triangle and Raised Anchor Wares* F. Lewis, Leigh-on-Sea 1948.

Mackintosh, Sir Harold *Early English Figure Pottery* Chapman and Hall, London 1938.

Mankowitz, Wolf *Wedgwood* Batsford, London 1953.

Marshall, H. Rissick *Coloured Worcester Porcelain of the First Period* The Ceramic Book Co., Newport, Mon. 1954.

McCauley, Robert H. *Liverpool Transfer Designs on Anglo-American Pottery* The Southworth-Anthoensen Press, Portland, Maine 1942.

Nance, E. Morton *The Pottery and Porcelain of Swansea and Nantgarw* Batsford, London 1942.

Partington, James R. *A History of Chemistry,* Vols.1-4 Macmillan, London 1962.

Plot, Robert *The Natural History of Staffordshire* Oxford 1686.

Price, E. Stanley *John Sadler, A Liverpool Pottery Printer* Published by the author, West Kirby, Cheshire 1948.

Price, Robert K. *Astbury, Whieldon, and Ralph Wood Figures and Toby Jugs* Bodley Head, London 1922.

Rackham, Bernard *Catalogue of the Schreiber Collection,* Vol.I—Porcelain, Vol.II—Earthenware. Board of Education, London 1930.

Rackham, Bernard *Medieval English Pottery* Faber and Faber, London 1948.

Read, Herbert *Staffordshire Pottery Figures* Duckworth, London and Houghton Mifflin, Boston and New York 1929.

Rice, Dennis G. *The Illustrated Guide to Rockingham Pottery and Porcelain* Barrie & Jenkins, London and Praeger, New York 1971.

Sandon, Henry *Worcester Porcelain 1751-1793* Herbert Jenkins, London 1969.

Shaw, J. T. ed. *The Potteries of Sunderland and District,* 3rd rev. edn. County Borough of Sunderland, Sunderland 1968.

Shaw, Simeon *The Chemistry of the Several Natural and Artificial Heterogeneous Compounds Used in Manufacturing Porcelain, Glass and Pottery* W. Lewis & Son, London 1837.

Shaw, Simeon *History of the Staffordshire Potteries* G. Jackson, Hanley 1829.

Smith, Alan *The Illustrated Guide to Liverpool Herculaneum Pottery* Barrie & Jenkins, London 1970.

Taggart, Ross E. *The Frank P. and Harriet C. Burnap Collection of English Pottery,* enlarged and rev. edn. Nelson Gallery-Atkins Museum, Kansas City, Missouri 1967.

Towner, Donald C. *English Cream-Coloured Earthenware* Pitman, New York 1957.

Towner, Donald C. *The Leeds Pottery* Cory, Adams & Mackay, London 1963.

Turner, Elizabeth *The Cowslip or More Cautionary Stories in Verse* 1811.

Turner, William *Transfer Printing on Enamels, Porcelain and Pottery* Chapman and Hall, London 1907.

Watkins, C. Malcolm *North Devon Pottery and Its Export to America in the 17th Century* United States National Museum Bulletin, No.225, Smithsonian Institution, Washington D.C. 1960.

The Ninth Wedgwood International Seminar, 1964 The Wedgwood International Seminar, New York 1971.

Whiter, Leonard *Spode* Barrie & Jenkins, London and Praeger, New York 1970.

Articles

Le Corbeiller, Clare 'Miss America and Her Sisters: Personifications of the Four Parts of the World' *Metropolitan Museum of Art* Bulletin, April 1961, pp.209-23.

Leon, Jack. L. 'Yellow-glazed English Earthenware', *Transactions of the English Ceramic Circle* (London 1971), Vol.8, Part I, pp.31-41.

Magriel, Paul 'Pugilism in English Pottery', *Antiques,* January 1948, pp.58-9.

Noël Hume, Ivor 'Creamware to Pearlware: A Williamsburg Perspective', *Ceramics in America* Univ. Press of Va., 1973.

Rackham, Bernard 'Early Tudor Pottery', *Transactions of the English Ceramic Circle* (London 1939), Vol.2, No.6, pp.15-25 (p.21 shows a yellow-glazed tile).

Stretton, E. Norman 'Thomas Rothwell, Engraver and Copper Plate Printer 1740-1807', *Transactions of the English Ceramic Circle* (London 1967), Vol.6, Part 3, pp.249-53.

Appendix

Some recipes for yellow glaze

1

Lawrence Harrison of Liverpool, 1767

    Litharge   9
    Antimony   6
    Lead & Tin Ashes 3
    Burnt in a Biscuit Dish at top of a Potters Kiln, when it wines out pound it, and put it in again three times over.

From E. Stanley Price, *John Sadler, A Liverpool Pottery Printer* (West Kirby, Cheshire 1948), p.89.

2

Benjamin Tomkinson of Liverpool, probably dating from the 1820s

    3 lb. Red Lead
    3 lb. Tin
    3 lb. Antimony

    Calcine the whole. This glaze will run very soon and give a good yellow.
From a photograph (Manuscript Collections, Liverpool Museum, courtesy of Alan Smith) of a page from Benjamin Tomkinson's notebook, which is part of 'The Tomkinson Papers'. These are a group of notebooks, recipes, etc., pertaining to the Herculaneum Pottery.
From Alan Smith, *The Liverpool Herculaneum Pottery* (Barrie & Jenkins, London 1970), p.23 and Appendix III.

3

Thomas Lakin

PROCESS 52
To Make a Yellow Underglaze
Take 4 parts of Raw Litharge
Take 3 parts of Crude Antimony
Take $1\frac{1}{2}$ parts of Oxide of Tin

Recipe for underglaze yellow taken from *The Valuable Receipts of The Late Mr Thomas Lakin* (published by Mrs Lakin, 1824) (Victoria and Albert Museum Library).

4

Recipe for a yellow glaze taken from William Evens, *Art and History of the Potting Business* (Shelton, 1846).

RECEIPT FOR YELLOW
Yellow calyx	14
Litharge	14
Frittglaze	72
Raw glaze	80

5

The Evens book also contains an Appendix and two inserted pages giving a number of yellow glaze recipes of 'Bailiff Thomas' and 'Bailiff John'

For 'NAPLES YELLOW'
White Lead	75
Oxide of Antimony	14
Mur. of Ammonia	7
Sulp. Potass. of Alumine	4

Index

References to figures are shown in italic, to colour plates in roman.